Love Addict

Love Addict

Mark G. Boyer,
Corbin S. Cole,
and Matthew S. Ver Miller

WIPF & STOCK · Eugene, Oregon

Wipf & Stock
An Imprint of Wipf and Stock Publishers
199 W. 8th Ave., Suite 3
Eugene, OR 97401

www.wipfandstock.com

PAPERBACK ISBN: 978-1-5326-6589-9
HARDCOVER ISBN: 978-1-5326-6590-5
EBOOK ISBN: 978-1-5326-6591-2

Manufactured in the U.S.A.   03/28/19

Dedicated to
Jesse Lee and Verna Marie Boyer
Jeffory Stan and Melissa Ann Cole
Michael Dean and Patricia Anne Miller

"The essence of love is to affectively affirm as well as to unselfishly delight in the well-being of others, and to engage in acts of care and service on their behalf; unlimited love extends this love to all others without exceptions in an enduring and constant way.... [U]nlimited love is often deemed a Creative Presence underlying and integral to all of reality; participation in unlimited love constitutes the fullest experience of spirituality."

—STEPHEN G. POST

Contents

Abbreviations

BCE = Before the Common Era (same as BC = Before Christ)
CE = Common Era (same as AD = *Anno Domini,* in the year of the Lord)

CB (NT) = Christian Bible (New Testament)

Acts = Acts of the Apostles
Col = Letter to the Colossians
1 Cor = First Letter of Paul to the Corinthians
2 Cor = Second Letter of Paul to the Corinthians
Eph = Letter to the Ephesians
Gal = Letter of Paul to the Galatians
Heb = Letter to the Hebrews
Jas = Letter of James
John = John's Gospel
1 John = First Letter of John
2 John = Second Letter of John
3 John = Third Letter of John
Jude = Letter of Jude
Luke = Luke's Gospel
Mark = Mark's Gospel
Matt = Matthew's Gospel
1 Pet = First Letter of Peter
2 Pet = Second Letter of Peter
Phil = Letter of Paul to the Philippians

Phlm = Letter of Paul to Philemon
Rev = Revelation
Rom = Letter of Paul to the Romans
1 Thess = First Letter of Paul to the Thessalonians
2 Thess = Second Letter of Paul to the Thessalonians
1 Tim = First Letter to Timothy
2 Tim = Second Letter to Timothy
Titus = Letter to Titus

HB (OT) = Hebrew Bible (Old Testament)

Deut = Deuteronomy
Isa = Isaiah
Lev = Leviticus

Notes on the Bible

The Bible

THE BIBLE IS DIVIDED into two parts: The Hebrew Bible (Old Testament) and the Christian Bible (New Testament). The Hebrew Bible, often referred to as the Old Testament, consists of thirty-nine named books accepted by Jews and Protestants as Holy Scripture. The Christian Bible, consisting of twenty-seven named books, is also called the New Testament; it is accepted by Christians as Holy Scripture. Thus, in this work:

—Hebrew Bible (Old Testament), abbreviated HB (OT), indicates that a book is found in the Hebrew Bible (Old Testament);

—and Christian Bible (New Testament), abbreviated CB (NT), indicates that a book is found only in the Christian Bible or New Testament.

In notating biblical texts, the first number refers to the chapter in the book, and the second number refers to the verse within the chapter. Thus, HB (OT) Isa 7:11 means that the quotation comes from Isaiah, chapter 7, verse 11. CB (NT) Mark 6:2 means that the quotation comes from Mark's Gospel, chapter 6, verse 2. When more than one sentence appears in a verse, the letters a, b, c, etc. indicate the sentence being referenced in the verse. Thus, HB (OT) 2 Kgs 1:6a means that the quotation comes from the Second Book of Kings, chapter 1, verse 6, sentence 1.

In the HB (OT), the reader often sees LORD (note all capital letters). Because God's name (Yahweh or YHWH, referred to as the Tetragrammaton) is not to be pronounced, the name Adonai (meaning *Lord*) is substituted for Yahweh when a biblical text is read. When a biblical text is translated and printed, LORD (cf. Gen 2:4) is used to alert the reader to what the text actually states: Yahweh. Furthermore, when the biblical author writes Lord Yahweh, printers present Lord GOD (note all capital letters for GOD; cf. Gen 15:2) to avoid the printed ambiguity of LORD LORD. When the reference is to Jesus, the word printed is Lord (note capital L and lower case letters; cf. Luke 11:1). When writing about a lord (note all lower case letters [cf. Matt 18:25]) with servants, no capital L is used.

Biblical Presuppositions

In the Christian Bible (New Testament), the oldest gospel is Mark's account of Jesus' victory. The author of Matthew's Gospel copied and shortened about eighty percent of Mark's material into his book and then added other stories to make the work longer. The author of Luke's Gospel copied and shortened about fifty percent of Mark's material into his orderly account and then added other stories to make the work much longer. The author of Luke's Gospel also wrote the Acts of the Apostles; this book serves as the second volume of a two-volume work and should be read in relationship with volume one: Luke's Gospel. John's Gospel is not related to the Synoptics (Mark, Matthew, Luke); it comes from a separate tradition often referenced as a school or community of authors.

Mark's Gospel begins as oral story-telling about Jesus of Nazareth, lasting for about forty years in that form. An unidentified author, called Mark for the sake of convenience, collects the oral stories, sets a plot, and writes the first gospel around 70 CE. Because Jesus was expected to return soon, no one had thought about recording what he had said and done until Mark came along and realized that he was not returning as quickly as had been thought. About ten years (80 CE) after Mark finished his gospel, Matthew needed to adopt Mark's narrative—originally intended for a peasant Gentile readership—to a Jewish audience. And about twenty years (90 CE) after Mark finished his gospel, Luke needed to adapt Mark's poor-Gentile intended work for a rich, upper class, urban, Gentile readership. The authors of John's Gospel (100 CE) did not know the existence of the other three works collectively named gospels.

Furthermore, gospels were not first intended to be read privately as is done today. They were meant to be heard in a group. The very low rate of literacy in the first century would have never dictated many copies of texts since most people could not read and their standard practice was to listen to another read the stories to them. Thus, what began as oral story-telling passed on by word of mouth became written story-telling preserved in gospels. A careful reading of Mark's Gospel will reveal the orality still embedded in the text, especially evident in the repetition of words and the organization of stories in three parts. In rewriting Mark's Gospel, Matthew and Luke remove the last traces of oral story-telling.

When it comes to Paul's Letters, there are genuine epistles and second-generation epistles. Genuine Pauline letters include Romans, 1 and 2 Corinthians, Galatians, Philippians, 1 Thessalonians, and Philemon. Second-generation Pauline letters are those written by someone in the name of Paul to deal with then-current issues after Paul's death around 64 CE; these include Ephesians, Colossians, 2 Thessalonians, 1 and 2 Timothy, and Titus. Second-generation Pauline letters contain much of Paul's thought, but they also move forward his theology for the next generation of followers of Jesus. Hebrews, even though it is identified as a letter, is better named a homily or sermon on Jesus as high priest, and it is not written by Paul.

Other CB (NT) letters, such as James, 1 and 2 Peter, and Jude are written in the name of someone famous in the Christian community to address those living into the second century CE. The letters of John—1, 2, and 3—like the Gospel of John, emerge out of a school or community of believers who share the same basic theology at the beginning of the second century CE. While it may seem odd to readers today, in the ancient world it was a common practice to attach the name of someone famous or well-known to a work in order to give it credibility. Thus, letters are often attributed to famous first-century Christians who were long dead when their letters were written.

Introduction

Another Book on Love

THIS IS ANOTHER BOOK on love! While the shelves of bookstores contain thousands of titles with the word *love* in them, this work takes that over-used word to a new understanding by surveying the use made of it by Christian Bible (New Testament) authors. In Greek, the language of the CB (NT), there are four words for love and each of those is examined below. No matter what the Greek word is, the English equivalent is always *love*, because there is only one word for love in the English language. This fact alone renders all English translations less than accurate. Furthermore, the word *love* can mean anything and everything. Two people love each other, but they also love pizza, beer, and potato chips. The word *love* is printed on T-shirts, billboards, and web pages—sometimes with the o slightly leaning to the right! "I love that dress" goes hand-in-hand with "I love my spouse." This overuse of the word *love*, coupled with the fact that one English word translates four distinct Greek words, leaves the reader wondering what is meant by love in a biblical text.

Jacob D. Myers makes an important point for our consideration here. In *Making Love with Scripture*, he states, ". . . [T]he word of God cannot be contained or constrained by the words of Scripture."[1] He means that the reader, who does not know Greek,

1. Myers, *Making Love*, 104.

must discover exactly what the word of God is attempting to communicate. And while he or she does so, the person must be fully aware that English—or any other language—cannot contain or constrain what God wishes to reveal. Our experiences of God reveal God—not words! Paul gets at this in his First Letter to the Corinthians, writing, ". . . We speak of these things in words not taught by human wisdom but taught by the Spirit, interpreting spiritual things to those who are spiritual" (1 Cor 2:13). In other words, reading the Bible is work. Sometimes, as in the case of this book, writers do most of the work for us. As the reader will see, we have combed the CB (NT) in order to present the non-contained and non-constrained word of God as it pertains to love.

As Paul states, we attempt to interpret spiritual things to those who are spiritual. There is no difference between a spiritual life and spirituality. Those living a spiritual life are connected to God through the Spirit. Their spirit has a lifeline to the Spirit, who transforms them gradually through divine love. Spirituality, the quality or the condition of being spiritual, is a process of transformation of the whole person into authentic biblical love, the highest form being self-sacrificial or agape love. Jesus taught the transformation of the whole person. Agape love transforms us or changes us from self-centered to selfless, from not caring to compassion, from judging to understanding, from a world separated from God to one united to, manifesting, and incarnating God. In other words, practicing the way of love taught by Jesus is nothing other than a school of love. This book should be included in the curriculum.

Gregory Polan reminds us that there exists "a distinctive way of listening—with the ear of the heart."[2] He states that "words come into our eyes and then flow down to our hearts."[3] This is the stance that we must take when contemplating Scripture. "The heart is the place where our human will, our mind, our deepest convictions, and our passions come together," states Polan.[4] This makes con-

---

2. Polan, "Final Address," 3.

3. Ibid.

4. Ibid.

templation nothing other than looking at reality with a primary gaze of love, according to Richard Rohr.[5] Matthew Lee, referencing Pitrim Sorokin, calls this love energy that is "commonly generated through the interaction of human beings."[6] According to Sorokin, ". . . [L]ove can be viewed as one of the highest energies known."[7] As we will show below, the great commandment of loving God, neighbor, and self—as taught by Jesus—"requires acute agape—love even to the point of loving one's enemies."[8] When we love as Jesus taught, "We find that giving ourselves to another in companionship and support does not diminish us," states John Shea. "In fact, the more we give ourselves to another to increase their being, the more our own sense of being increases. We become who we are by giving ourselves to another."[9] Thus, love in all its Greek-word connotations serves as a lens through which the Bible can be read and interpreted. According to Myers, "[Love] approaches the other [and the Other] barefooted, because the space love opens up between the self and the other [and the Other] is holy ground."[10] According to Rohr, "Love utterly redefines the nature of power. Power without love is mere brutality, and love without power is only the sentimentality of private lives disconnected from the Whole."[11] Nevertheless, according to Myers, "Love is wild. It cannot be tamed, nor does it aim to tame the other."[12] In the CB (NT) Jesus is the best example of wild, acute, and addictive love. The Fourth Eucharistic Prayer in *The Roman Missal* captures it this way: ". . . [W]hen the hour had come for [our Lord Jesus Christ] to be glorified by [the] Father . . . , having loved his own who were in the world, he loved them to the end . . . ."[13]

5. Rohr, "Irreplaceable 'Thisness.'"

6. Lee, *Heart*, 99.

7. Ibid., 200.

8. Ibid., 205.

9. Shea, *Dare*, 87.

10. Myers, *Making Love*, 118.

11. Rohr, "Breach-Menders."

12. Myers, *Making Love*, 147.

13. *Roman Missal*, "Order of Mass," par. 119.

Greek Love

In the language of the CB (NT)—Greek—there are four words for love. Greek's richness turns into English's poorness with its one word for love. The depth of CB (NT) nuance is lost when all English translators have to work with is love. This book, *Love Addict*, attempts to remedy this illness.

Agape

The most used Greek word for love in the CB (NT) is *agape* (ah-gah-peh), the noblest word for love in Greek. Agape is used to describe God's very nature as well as the delight we get when sacrificing ourselves for the greater good of another or others. This type of love continues to love even when a person gets no immediate response; it is unconditional love. It seeks no reward, only wanting to give away the self. Such love of esteem or valuation desires only the good of the beloved. This is not a feeling type of love, but a doing type of love—an exercise of the will, a deliberate choice, commitment. Agape wills the good of another or others for the sake of another or others.

The English word *agape* is derived from *agape*; it means wide open. For example, the door of the room was agape. Or, upon hearing the good news, a person's mouth was agape, that is, wide open. The surprise or wonder associated with agape is imbedded in agape, which is selfless love for others. Agape is also used to describe the earliest Christian community meal in commemoration of the Lord's Supper because it not only demonstrated the self-sacrifice of Christ, but because it represented the openness of the members of the community to fellow members and to others (Jude 1:12).

Philia

The second most used word for love in the CB (NT) is *philia* (fee-lee-a). This is brotherly or sisterly affectionate love between equals, that is, those of the same blood. *Philia* refers to devotion to, fondness for, or liking another. It desires to receive as well as to give; it implies a strong emotional connection. As friendship love, it can be understood as kindness or appreciation or the pleasure we take in a person. It indicates a special interest in someone or something. Thus, *philia* can also refer to the delight we get when seeing a painting or sculpture, listening to a song, enjoying a tasty meal, delighting in a sweet scent, or experiencing the sensation of a relaxing massage.

In English we find *philia* in Philadelphia, the city of brotherly love. We also find it in philanthropy, the love for humanity with a corresponding demonstration of benevolence, usually in terms of monetary contributions. Likewise, we know that a philanderer is a person who loves to flirt with the opposite sex. And philosophy is, of course, a love of wisdom.

Storge

The third word for love in Greek is *storge*, which is used only several times in the CB (NT). *Storge* (store-gay) refers to love that is based in one's nature. It is natural affection, such as the natural movement of husband towards wife, of parents toward children, or of owner towards a pet. It can be used to reference the love a person has for his or her country or favorite sports team. In the CB (NT) it usually appears in a negative form, meaning without this type of love.

The word *storge* is used in British English to denote the natural or instinctive affection of a parent for a child. In United States English, we are not aware of its use, since it does not appear in the 1999 *Encarta: World English Dictionary*.

Eros

The fourth Greek word for love is *eros* (eh-raw-s), which does not appear in the CB (NT). It is the love of sexual passion, emotional involvement based on body chemistry, intimate love, romantic love. It is all about sexual self-satisfaction from another person that pleases another one. This type of love leads to marriage, maybe procreating or adopting children, and the formation of deep, long-lasting bonds of strength and trust between two people. Thus, it leads to an appreciation for the beauty within a person that may lead to an appreciation for beauty itself.

The Greeks worshiped Eros, the goddess of sexual love. Eros makes its way into English as erotic, someone or something that arouses sexual feelings of desire. Art or literature intended to do this is often referred to as erotica, whereas the quality is the noun *eroticism* with its verb *to eroticize*.

Greek Forms

In English, love can function as a noun (love) or a verb (to love, loved, loving); so, too, in Greek. In English, lovely and beloved serve as adjectives; so, too, in Greek. In order to avoid transliterating the many Greek word-forms using *agape*, *philia*, and *storge* into English, we have chosen to standardize our usage. When writing about self-sacrificial love in any of its grammatical uses, including noun, verb, or adjective, we will use *agape*. When writing about friendship, brotherly, or sisterly love in any of its grammatical uses, we will use *philia*. And for the few times that natural love appears, we will use *storge*. Our desire is to present the types of love mentioned in the CB (NT) and reflect upon them without getting bogged down in Greek word-forms and grammar.

This Book

Love Addict, the title of this book, is meant to be both paradoxical and oxymoronic. A paradox is a statement that appears to be contradictory, but upon careful examination reveals a depth of truth. Thus, love, with its multiple definitions and compound-word creations, has an addictive quality. People crave love, just like they crave reward and reinforcement through drugs and compulsive or obsessive behaviors and are physiologically and/or neurologically dependent on it. Furthermore, since an addict can be a person who is enthusiastically devoted or surrendered to something, we have another paradox in terms of devotion to love.

An oxymoron is a phrase in which two words of contradictory meaning are used together for special effect. *Love Addict*, referring to a person addicted to love, makes the title oxymoronic. We do not think of ourselves as addicts when thinking about the person we love, nor do we consider those who love us as addicts.

Both with its paradoxical and oxymoronic meanings this book explores the uses of love in the CB (NT) in an effort to mine the truths that are buried in those ancient words and phrases. In order to accomplish this feat, we use the following five-part exercise in fifteen-minute spirituality.

The first part is the name or title of the section broadly placed within six chapters, each of which illustrates a theme.

The second part of each exercise is a short quotation from Scripture, which contains the mention of the word *love*.

The reflection, part three, explores the meaning of love in its biblical context in several paragraphs. After identifying the Greek word being used for love in the Scripture passage, it attempts to make some application for today based on its biblical context. Each entry consists of two paragraphs, which make it thorough, readable, and to the point. It is built upon images that love evokes within its biblical book context, and it is designed to help the reader come to a deeper understanding of biblical love.

In the journal/meditation section, part four, the reader makes connections between the title, the Scripture passage, the reflection, and his or her own life. These connections may be written in a journal—either paper or electronic—or meditated on with the help of the question. The journal/meditation question gets one started; where the journal/meditation goes cannot be predetermined. It may be a single statement or an idea with which one lingers for a few minutes, a few hours, or a few days. The process has no end; the reader decides when he or she has finished exploring the topic.

Once the reader is finished, the exercise is concluded with a short prayer, part five. The prayer summarizes the love announced in the title and Scripture, which was explored in the reflection, and which served as the foundation for the journal/meditation. Each prayer addresses God in praise of divine love and petitions the Holy One to lead the pray-er into deeper love.

We know that God is neither male nor female, but to avoid repetition of proper names for God, we have chosen to use the masculine pronouns in reflections and prayers. Also, masculine pronouns are used often in English translations.

The five-part process is an exercise in spirituality, that is, growth in wisdom and grace. Spirituality, as a way of life, transforms or transfigures a person step-by-step as he or she gets closer and closer to the divine—however one chooses to name it. After meeting the divine, the individual better understands some of the circumstances of his or her life, including his or her unique self. Spirituality is the way one is in the divine's presence, which emerges through human experiences of biblical authors writing about love and guided reflections upon those experiences by us, the authors of this book.

Our hope is that you, the reader, will grow in spirituality through these reflections on love. Our prayer is that you will finish this spiritual journey enriched for having spent time with *Love Addict*.

Mark G. Boyer
Corbin S. Cole
Matthew S. Ver Miller

1

Love and God

God Is Love

Scripture: ". . . [E]veryone who loves is born of God and knows God. Whoever does not love does not know God, for God is love." (1 John 4:7b–8)

Reflection: The Greek word for love used in the above quotation is agape, which delights in giving. This self-sacrificing love holds the object of love in high esteem. Because it delights in self-sacrifice, it keeps on loving even when the one loved fails to respond. In other words, agape is unconditional love. The author of the First Letter of John uniquely writes that "God is love." God delights in giving himself to us. God takes great pleasure in sharing who he is with his creation. In fact, God self-sacrifices himself—and takes great delight in doing so—because he gets great pleasure from loving even when we, the object of his love, fail to respond. God never stops loving, as it is his very nature to do so.

The author of the First Letter of John repeats himself a few verses later, declaring again, "God is love" (1 John 4:16b). Then, he adds, "and those who abide in love abide in God, and God abides in them" (1 John 16:b). This means that the God who is love finds

LOVE ADDICT

us acceptable or worthy of his love and is willing to await a response from us. While he waits, he continues to live in us, to reside
in us. Even if we do not respond to God's love, our lack of response
does not remove the fact that God's essence is self-sacrificing love.
God's very being is love, according to the author of the First Letter
of John. God as love is revealed to us through Christ, whose death
shows us the very nature of God as love. God never stops giving
away himself because it is his very nature to do so.

Journal/Meditation: In what specific ways have you experienced God's love? What response did you make? Is there a time
when you were unresponsive to God, who loved you anyway?

Prayer: O God, you are love, and those who abide in love
abide in you and you abide in them. I praise you for your delight in
loving me and ask that you continue today, tomorrow, and forever
and ever. Amen.

Source of Love

Scripture: "Beloved, let us love one another, because love is from
God . . . ." (1 John 4:7a)

Reflection: Because God is love, God is the source of love
poured into creation. The self-sacrificing God freely shares his love
with everything he made. Earlier in his First Letter, John exclaims,
"See what love the Father has given us, that we should be called
children of God" (1 John 3:1a). In other words, the origin of all
love, God, changes us by his love for us. Just as the love of one
person for another changes the other, when God loves, people are
changed by the source of love. In his Letter to the Romans, Paul
writes about "God's love [that] has been poured into our hearts
through the Holy Spirit that has been given to us" (Rom 5:5). For
the apostle, the vehicle of God's love is the Holy Spirit. ". . . God
proves his love for us," writes Paul, "in that while we still were sin-
ners Christ died for us" (Rom 5:8). If anyone needs proof that God
loves people, the death of his own Son should be evidence enough.

In the second-generation Pauline Letter to the Ephesians, the
author elaborates on God's love. He writes that "God, who is rich

in mercy, out of the great love with which he loved us even when we were dead through our trespasses, made us alive together with Christ . . ." (Eph 2:4–5). Even sin cannot stop God from loving people. God's giving of his love from himself as the source of all love changes them. At the end of the letter, the author wishes peace to the whole community of readers "and love with faith, from God the Father and the Lord Jesus Christ" (Eph 6:23). As the source of love, God's agape, his own nature, releases people from deadly sin and raises them to life.

Journal/Meditation: In what specific ways have you experienced God's unmerited, undeserved, great love? How did those experiences change you?

Prayer: God, source of all love poured into people's hearts through your Holy Spirit, you bring people to life even though they may be dead in sin. Change my heart with even greater love that flows outward to those around me forever and ever. Amen.

Love Is Greatest

Scripture: ". . . [N]ow faith, hope, and love abide, these three; and the greatest of these is love." (1 Cor 13:13)

Reflection: There is no doubt that Paul considers love to be the greatest gift from God because God is love, and because God is the source of love. This understanding leads the apostle to reflect upon the great gifts God gives to people—such as eloquent speech, extraordinary knowledge, and voluntary poverty—and to declare that without love he is nothing. To love, Paul attributes patience, kindness, and truth. There is no room for envy, boasting, arrogance, rudeness, stubbornness, irritableness, resentfulness, or wrongdoing. "It bears all things, believes all things, hopes all things, endures all things" (1 Cor 13:7). In other words, "Love never ends" (1 Cor 13:8a). Love never ends because its source is the eternal God.

The author of the second-generation Pauline letter to the Colossians understands unending love to be the glue that binds together all people. "Above all," he writes to his readers, "clothe yourselves with love, which binds everything together in perfect harmony" (Col 3:14). If the members of his community put on love the same way they put on their clothes, they will go out of their way self-sacrificially for each other. By putting the other person first—which means that everyone is holding everyone in the highest of esteem—the result is perfect harmony in the community. It is imitating God, who is love and the source of love. It continues the process of giving away love. God gives his love to us, and we give it to each other. That is what makes love endure. That is what makes love the greatest of all things.

Journal/Meditation: In what specific ways have you given away the love that God gave to you? In what specific ways have you received the love from another person that was given to him or her by God?

Prayer: O God, your love is patient, kind, and truthful, bearing all things, believing all things, hoping all things, and enduring all things. Grant me a deeper share in your love that never ends now and forever. Amen.

God Loves Us First

Scripture: "In this is love, not that we loved God but that he loved us . . . ." (1 John 4:10)

Reflection: God loves us self-sacrificially writes the author of the First Letter of John. He exhorts us to "[s]ee what love the Father has given us" (1 John 3:1), and he reminds us that "[w]e love because he first loved us" (1 John 4:19) if we know "and believe the love that God has for us" (1 John 4:16). The reason we are able to love is because God loves us first. "[O]ut of the great love with which he loved us" (Eph 2:4), we discover that we cannot not love. In a manner of speaking, we are forced into agape or self-sacrificing love because God loves us first with a love greater than we can ever muster. Just like when someone takes a chance on us—like a CEO accepting an employee's idea or a minister accepting a congregant's suggestion for a sermon—God risks loving us. We don't deserve God's love. We cannot earn it, bargain for it, or negotiate it. God decides without consulting us to risk pouring divine love into us. This divine love with which the All-loving One graces us is a shock. God's love stuns us with love. Furthermore, God does not love us if we change; in fact, our faults and weaknesses bring us to the Father. God is not interested in perfection and strength; he seems to have a fondness to love us into change. God's love sparks—and sometimes even sets on fire—our inner transformation. Thus, only love is real, and only love endures throughout life, through death, and into everlasting life with the source of love: God. In loving us first, the Mighty One enables us to return love with the giver's own love. Unless God loves us first, we cannot respond to the love shared by the Father, the Son, and the Holy Spirit. Such divine love enables us to pass from this life through death to that eternal love, where we and God disappear as others and unite as one.

Journal/Meditation: What is your response to God first loving you? In what specific ways has God taken a chance on you?

Prayer: Father, I see what love you have given me, and I believe in the great love with which you have first loved me. Continue to bring me through one transformation after another until you perfect your love in me today and into eternity. Amen.

Keep Yourself in Love

Scripture: ". . . I am convinced that neither death, nor life, nor angels, nor rulers, no things present, nor things to come, nor powers, nor height, nor depth, nor anything else in all creation, will be able to separate us from the love of God . . . ." (Rom 8:38–39)

Reflection: Unlike Jude who tells his readers to keep themselves "in the love of God" (Jude 1:21)—implying that there may be ways to fall out of it—Paul tells the Romans about his conviction that nothing is able to separate people from the love of God. Jude, it seems, presumes more free will than Paul is willing to give! For Paul, agape love is participating in divine life. God wills himself for people, who, when they want nothing more than the Holy One's will, consummate their union in self-sacrificing love. The task is to discern where our wills and the Mighty-one's will are at variance and bring our desires into conformity with God's, especially our ultimate destiny to be incorporated into perfect love.

Love is a conscious decision. Actual love is a highly conscious act. Once we know that the origin of all love is God, that the Holy One loves us first and desires that we respond in kind with the great love with which he has loved us, and we do respond, then we are participating in divine love from which nothing in creation can separate us. So, we keep ourselves in the love of God by loving God. It is only through the love of the All-loving One that we can present ourselves in a pleasing manner to the very Holy One who loved us first. Thus, there is an energy of love that we can harness. This energy surpasses all other sources of energy. It is greater than water, wind, fossil fuels, or sun. Divine love not only keeps us in God's love, but it prohibits anything from separating us from it.

Journal/Meditation: How do you keep yourself in the love of God? To what do you compare divine love? What is it like?

Prayer: All-loving God, nothing can separate me from your love. Continue to keep me in your love today, tomorrow, and into eternity. Amen.

Love God

Scripture: "No one has ever seen God; if we love one another, God lives in us, and his love is perfected in us." (1 John 4:12)

Reflection: Because God is spirit, we cannot see the Eternal One. Yet the invisible Holy One desires to establish a relationship with each of us. If our response to the All-loving One's offer is affirmative, then we manifest love for God by loving another or others. In other words, if we accept the offer of the invisible relationship with God, we make it visible through our love of others. We cannot see love; love is invisible. No one can give us a cup of love. However, we can see the person we love, the beloved, who becomes a sign of God's love in us. We can feel the love of another person in a one-on-one relationship and in corporate worship and nature. Our experiences of love through another, through others, through nature bring us into a culture of love where we get a little experience of "[w]hat no eyes has seen, nor ear heard, nor the human heart conceived, what God has prepared for those who love him" (1 Cor 2:9).

This taste of love in the First Letter of John begets the self-sacrificing culture of love. It sparks obedience to God's word which indicates that "the love of God has reached perfection" in us (1 John 2:5). This is agape love in action, putting the other or others first and being committed to their good. "By this we know that we love the children of God," writes First John, "when we love God and obey his commandments. For the love of God is this, that we obey his commandments. And his commandments are not burdensome . . ." (1 John 5:2–3). As God's love is reaching perfection in us, we are loving others whether we feel like it or not; we have transcended feelings and are doing the right thing for no reason other than it is the right thing to do. It is hard to love unconditionally, because the temptation is to give into feelings. "Blessed is anyone who endures temptation," writes James. "Such a one has stood the test and will receive the crown of life that the Lord has promised to those who love him" (Jas 1:12).

Journal/Meditation: Whom do you love self-sacrificially? How does he or she represent your love for God? How is love being perfected in you? How do you manifest God through love?

Prayer: No one has ever seen you, no one has ever heard you, no human heart has ever conceived of you, O God. Yet, if we love one another, you live in us, you give us a glimpse of what you have prepared for us, and your love is perfected in us now and forever. Amen.

2

Love, God, and the Son

God Loves the Son

Scripture: "The Father loves the Son and shows him all that he himself is doing, and he will show him greater works than these, so that you will be astonished." (John 5:20)

Reflection: The Greek word for love in John 5:20 is philia, which refers to love between equals. Thus, in this reflective section of John's Gospel, the Johannine Jesus is referring to his relationship with God. There is a friendship between the Father and Son; there is a desire both to give and to receive. In the verse preceding this one, the Johannine Jesus declares that the Son does nothing on his own; he does only what he sees the Father doing. There is a unity, a Father-Son relationship of give and take, such that Jesus states that the Father's love for the Son leads him to share with the Son all the Father is doing, even the greater work of resurrection from the dead. If that doesn't astonish anyone, then probably nothing will!

The mutual love of Father and Son, philia, is based on human father-son relationships. A father teaches carpentry to his son, who learns how to cut wood and drive nails. A father teaches his son how to play the guitar or another musical instrument. A father teaches his son how to play golf. A good older friend teaches a good younger friend the meaning of relationship. These activities, and others like them, illustrate the power and authority of a father sharing the same with his son. In other words, this is philia in action. Earlier in the gospel, the author states, "The Father loves the Son and has placed all things in his hands" (John 3:35). In this verse, the Greek word for love is agape, self-sacrificing love. Thus, John's Gospel presents a good blend between philia, relationship love between equals, and agape, self-sacrificing love.

Journal/Meditation: What have been your experiences of the blend of love that is both friendship- or relationship-oriented and self-sacrificial?

Prayer: Father, love me like you love your Son and show me all that you are doing, that I may bear witness to your greater works and be astonished in this life and all the way into eternal life. Amen.

God's Love Revealed in the Son

Scripture: "God's love was revealed among us in this way: God sent his only Son into the world so that we might live through him." (1 John 4:9)

Reflection: The author of the First Letter of John states that divine love became incarnate in Jesus. In his flesh, self-sacrificing love was born. Jesus was sacrificial love walking around, according to the First Letter of John. Thus, his very person revealed divine love; divine love appeared so that it could be heard, seen, and touched (1 John 1:1). Earlier in his First Letter, John states, "We know [agape] love by this, that [Jesus] laid down his life for us . . ." (1 John 3:16). This idea is very similar to John 3:16: "For God so loved the world that he gave his only Son . . . ." A similar sentiment is found in the Letter to the Ephesians, in which the author exhorts his readers to "be imitators of God . . . and live in love, as Christ loved us . . ." (Eph 5:2). The author of the Letter to Titus refers to this showing of love as the "loving kindness of God our Savior" (Titus 3:4). Titus, however, refers to love as good relationship love.

Love, revealed in Jesus, is human. The authors of CB (NT) books reflect upon divine love in human form. Thus, once Jesus is encountered, he calls for relationship, as Titus makes clear. This relationship gives us eternal life through Jesus (1 John 4:9; John 3:16). It also provides us with a model; because he laid down his life for us, we ought to lay down our lives for one another (1 John 3:16). This relationship enables us to live in the love of the One who gave himself for us as a sacrifice to God (Eph 5:2). And by living in that self-sacrificing love, we live in the essence of divine love. Our relationship with Jesus and our human, incarnate relationships with each other should reveal such divine, self-sacrificial love to others with whom we share both agape and philia, even to our enemies.

Journal/Meditation: In whom do you see incarnate, agape love? How do you reveal to others incarnate, agape love?

Prayer: O God, you so loved the world that you gave your only Son in whom you revealed your love. Grant that everyone who believes in him may manifest your love and have eternal life. Amen.

Jesus Loves the Father

Scripture: Jesus said, ". . . I do as the Father has commanded me, so that the world may know that I love the Father." (John 14:31a)

Reflection: Jesus, incarnate love, comes from the Father, yet as the author of John's Gospel makes clear, he submits himself to God's will. Whatever the Father commands him to do, he does it. In fact, he tells his disciples: "If you keep my commandments, you will abide in my love, just as I have kept my Father's commandments and abide in his love" (John 15:10). The commandments referred to by Jesus are summarized in one world: love. This, of course, is self-sacrificing love, which presumes that a person does what God wants him or her to do. The unique Johannine word *abide* attempts to capture this concept. Abide means to live, to reside, to exist in. Thus, Jesus lives, resides, and exists in the agape love of the Father of which he is also incarnate. He offers the same possibility to us. If we keep his love, we abide in him and, simultaneously, because he abides in God, we abide in the Father.

This submissive, self-sacrificial love is like the existence of life in vines and branches. If the vine is severed from the branch, it dies because it no longer has its source of life. It is like a deep friendship; if friends do not make time for one another—this is, if either stops self-sacrifice—then neither is able to share or to receive the energetic love of the other. True marital relationships wither quickly without husband and wife abiding in each other's love. We see incarnate love abiding in those couples who have been married forty, fifty, or sixty years. Each person naturally wants to sacrifice himself or herself for the other; that desire to submit to abiding in the other's love reveals agape to each other, to the community in which the couple lives, and to the world, just like Jesus did.

Journal/Meditation: In whom do you abide in love? What submission is involved? What is this love like?

Prayer: Father, by keeping your command to love, your Son abides in your love. Grant me the grace to abide in Jesus' love through those I love, so that I may abide in your love now and forever. Amen.

Jesus Loves Us

Scripture: Jesus said to his disciples, ". . . [T]he Father himself loves you, because you have loved me and have believed that I came from God." (John 16:27)

Reflection: Every person wants to love another and to be loved by another; love seems to be woven onto the human DNA helix. Every person longs for unity with another or others because we share the same source of love: God. Divine love fills the universe and leads every individual to enjoy diversity, itself the creative result of love. However, love, once recognized as coming from another, also seeks its source. The Johannine Jesus states that the Father relates (philia) to Jesus' followers because they relate (philia) to him. This philia is like a chain; believers are linked to Jesus, and Jesus is linked to God. Thus, through Jesus, believers are linked to the Father, the source of love. This means that every person can be a manifestation of God's love because each is infinitely loved by God just like Jesus was and, through Jesus, linked to God. In other words, when believers love Jesus, they are also loving God and being loved by God.

The author of the Letter to the Ephesians prays that his readers will "know the love of Christ that surpasses knowledge, so that [they] may be filled with all the fullness of God" (Eph 3:19). This author uses agape, self-sacrificial love. He prays that people will be so immersed in agape, like Jesus, that they will be unable to articulate it. At that point they will be filled to overflowing in the fullness of God's love—a description of which is beyond human words. In other words, they will be revelators of God's love to each other. They will be walking mirrors that reflect God's self-sacrificing love to the world. If we look at them, we see God's love reflected back to us. And no words can begin to capture that experience.

Journal/Meditation: How have you immersed yourself into God's love? To whom have you most recently reflected God's and Jesus' love? How did you do so?

Prayer: Father, help me to comprehend the breadth and length and height and depth of the love of Jesus Christ that is beyond words and be filled with all the fullness of your love now and forever. Amen.

Those Jesus Loved

Scripture: "Jesus, looking at [the rich man], loved him and said, 'You lack one thing; go, sell what you own, and give the money to the poor, and you will have treasure in heaven; then come, follow me.'" (Mark 10:21)

Reflection: In the gospels, there are specific people Jesus is said to have loved. One of them is the rich man in Mark's Gospel. He wants to know how to inherit eternal life. The Markan Jesus tells him to keep the commandments, but he replies that he has done that. Then, Jesus not only loves him self-sacrificially, but he employs the power of that love to challenge the rich man to do the same. In fact, in his richness he lacks only one more step: He must remove what keeps him from having treasure in heaven; he must strip himself of his riches, give the proceeds to the poor, and follow Jesus. The Markan Jesus awakens the rich man to the power of self-sacrificial love! He doesn't test him; he doesn't rebuke him; he doesn't threaten him. He merely loves him. However, as Mark narrates the story, the man is not able to immerse himself in this love and be transformed by it (Mark 10:22). It is interesting that when the author of Matthew's Gospel and the author of Luke's Gospel copy this tale from Mark's Gospel, both of them omit the note about Jesus loving the young rich man (Matt 19:21) or Jesus loving the very rich ruler (Luke 18:22).

In John's Gospel, Jesus is said to have "loved Martha and her sister [Mary] and Lazarus" (John 11:5) in a self-sacrificial manner like he loves the Markan rich man. However, once Jesus discovers that Lazarus has died and goes to the tomb in which he is buried, the Jews, who have joined the sisters in mourning their dead brother, declare that Jesus loved Lazarus as a friend (philia) (John 11:36). The Johannine Jesus, love incarnate, is the conduit for divine, self-sacrificial love to be returned to Lazarus. This agape love has the power to bring life into his four-day-old dead body. Thus, if Jesus' incarnate love can call the dead Lazarus from his tomb, how much easier is it for God to raise Jesus and for the Trinity to raise us? As the author of John's Gospel makes clear, Jesus loved "his own who were in the world, [and] he loved them to the end" (John 13:1b). What Jesus did for Lazarus, the Father did for Jesus. And the Father, Son, and Spirit promise to do the same for us who are loved by the Trinity.

Journal/Meditation: What two or three people do you love self-sacrificially (agape)? What two or three people do you love as friends (philia)?

Prayer: Jesus, look at me and love me with the Father's self-sacrificial, transforming love that I may detach myself from all worldly things and enjoy treasure in heaven now and forever. Amen.

Beloved Disciple

Scripture: "One of [Jesus'] disciples—the one whom Jesus loved—was reclining next to him. So while reclining next to Jesus, he asked him, 'Lord, who is it?'" (John 13:23, 25)

Reflection: The disciple Jesus loved is a unique, unnamed character in John's Gospel. Sometimes referred to as the beloved disciple, he remains unnamed because he is a sign of one who is so loved self-sacrificially by Jesus that he believes. In the first edition of John's Gospel, this disciple Jesus loves makes three appearances. The first is at a supper Jesus eats with his disciples. The disciple reclines next to Jesus and asks him about whom he speaks when he tells them that one of them will betray him (John 13:21–22). His second appearance is at the cross, where the crucified Jesus entrusts his mother into the beloved disciple's care and the beloved disciple into her care (John 19:26–27). After finding the stone rolled away from Jesus' tomb, Mary Magdalene runs to Simon Peter and the disciple Jesus loved (philia)—here he is identified as Jesus' friend—to tell them what she has discovered (John 20:2); this is the third appearance of the beloved disciple. Throughout the rest of the narrative about Simon Peter and the beloved disciple going to the tomb, the disciple is referred to as "the other disciple" (John 20:3, 4, 8). What is important, however, is "he saw and believed" (John 20:8). He is a sign of any believer, anyone who loves Jesus self-sacrificially or as a friend. Through sharing food, he is united to Jesus. Through his presence at the cross, he is trustworthy. Through belief in Jesus' resurrection, he becomes the icon of anyone who sees and believes.

In a second edition of John's Gospel, another chapter was added to the original work. In this epilogue, "the disciple whom Jesus loved" (John 21:20) makes another appearance. His role in the epilogue is that of witness. First, from a boat "[t]hat disciple whom Jesus loved" (John 21:7) recognizes the risen Jesus standing on the beach. Second, he testifies to the truth of what is written in John's Gospel (John 21:20–24). In these last references, Jesus is said to love him self-sacrificially. This disciple, who is loved very much by Jesus, is also Jesus' friend. Sharing both types of love—agape and philia—he experiences wholeness, completeness, and fulfillment, and he is commissioned for the ministry of putting his quill to papyrus or, minimally, narrating his experiences of being loved by Jesus. Love that is willing to die for you and love that wants to relate to you make you a beloved disciple.

Journal/Meditation: In what ways are you a beloved disciple? What does it mean for you to be referred to as a disciple Jesus loves?

Prayer: Father, the love of Jesus was so strong in the disciple he loved that he was able to recognize the risen Christ as Lord. Grant that I may experience this love and be a witness to your mighty deeds today, tomorrow, and forever and ever. Amen.

Love Jesus Christ 1

Scripture: Jesus said to his disciples, "They who have my commandments and keep them are those who love me; and those who love me will be loved by my Father, and I will love them and reveal myself to them." (John 14:21)

Reflection: The Johannine Jesus presents a love-link from his followers, who keep his commandment to love, to him, and, through him, to the Father. Earlier he had stated to his disciples, "If you love me, you will keep my commandments" (John 14:15). He further emphasizes the link of love when he says, "Those who love me will keep my word, and my Father will love them, and we will come to them and make our home with them" (John 14:23). Earlier in the gospel, when addressing the Jews, Jesus spoke about the link of love, saying, "If God were your Father, you would love, for I came from God and now I am here. I did not come on my own, but he sent me" (John 8:42). Finally, in a prayer that concludes Jesus' last words to his disciples, he tells his Father that he has made known the Father's name to his followers so that the love with which the Father loves him may be in them and that he may be in them (John 17:26). This love-link from disciples to Jesus to the Father also moves from the Father to Jesus to disciples.

Keeping in mind that the author of John's Gospel perceives the world as dual—the world above where God lives and the world below where people live—love overcomes the duality. It links the two stories of the universe together. Love is the unconditional energy that gives life to all (from the Father through the Son to the people on earth) and is the same energy that flows from people through the Son to the Father. In other words, love is like the electric wire from the main line to a house with an electric generator or solar panels; the house receives electricity from the main line, but it also supplies electricity to the main line. Self-sacrificing love, according to the Johannine Jesus, links together people and God through Jesus.

Journal/Meditation: Where do you fit into the love-link? In what specific ways have you experienced the power of love?

Prayer: Righteous Father, Jesus has made your name known to me, and, through love, I make it known to others. Grant that the love with which you have loved me may be in them and I in them just as Jesus' self-sacrificial love is in me and I am in you through him now and forever. Amen.

Love Jesus Christ 2

Scripture: ". . . Jesus said to Simon Peter, 'Simon son of John, do you love me more than these?' He said to him, 'Yes, Lord, you know that I love you.' Jesus said to him, 'Feed my lambs.'" (John 21:15)

Reflection: There is no doubt that chapter 21 of John's Gospel is a later addition to the work. Commonly referred to as the epilogue, one of its purposes is to rehabilitate Simon Peter, who had three times denied knowing Jesus (John 18:17, 25–27). In the Jesus-Peter dialogue, Jesus asks Peter if he loves him self-sacrificially in the first and second of three questions (John 21:15–16). However, in the third question, Jesus asks Peter if he loves him as a friend. This is due to Peter's reply to Jesus' first and second question when he replies that he loves Jesus as a friend (John 21:15–16). In other words, after asking Peter if he loves him with agape love and getting two responses from Peter that he loves Jesus with philia love, Jesus changes the question to philia in order to get a third response of relationship love from Peter (John 21:17). This helps the reader understand why Peter feels hurt when Jesus asks him the third time if he loves him as a friend, since Peter had already told Jesus two times that he loved him as a friend. The Johannine Jesus, of course, wants more.

Because the beloved disciple seems to trump Peter's leadership role in John's Gospel, Peter, even though he is rehabilitated by his three-fold confession of love of Jesus, has not yet reached self-sacrificing love. Jesus moves a step down to Peter with relationship love. Jesus is willing to move to our human level whether we know it or not in order to connect with us. That is what his incarnation, his becoming human flesh, is about. Jesus knows that love grows. What begins as a casual meeting may turn into an occasional acquaintance, which, in turn, may become a friendship. After that, agape love may enter the relationship. Philia pulls us toward agape. While philia may be enough for us, Jesus' self-sacrificing love pulls us toward agape. That is why Jesus was questioning Peter. That is why Jesus questions us.

Journal/Meditation: Is your love for Jesus that of an equal friend or that of self-sacrifice? Do you resemble Peter or Jesus? Explain. How has Jesus pulled you toward agape love in your relationships?

Prayer: Jesus, I hear your question about my love for you and your command to demonstrate it by feeding others with that same love. Ask the Father to deepen my self-sacrificial love for you that I may serve others as you did today, tomorrow, and forever. Amen.

Love Jesus Christ 3

Scripture: "Who will separate us from the love of Christ?" (Rom 8:35a)

Reflection: According to Paul in his Letter to the Romans, once we are joined in self-sacrificial love to Christ, nothing can separate us from him. Paul's understanding is that God offered people a second opportunity to respond to him; the first

17

opportunity in Adam failed. Knowing that people are not able to approach God, Paul states that God approached people with himself, commonly called grace, and, thus, gave them the ability to respond to his offer of love. The man who demonstrated the perfect acceptance of God's grace was Christ Jesus, the new Adam, the anointed one, the person chosen by God to demonstrate how to respond to God's offer of grace-love. God justifies people; God declares people acceptable to himself. Thus, in Pauline thought, God has withheld nothing from people. God's self-sacrificial love is so strong that no one or nothing can separate us from the love of Christ. This is what the author of the Second Letter to Timothy means when he tells his readers, "Hold to the standard of sound teaching that you have heard . . . in the faith and love that are in Christ Jesus" (2 Tim 1:13). For us, sound teaching is found in the plurality of the twenty-seven books of the CB (NT). Only God can withdraw his love; nothing outside of God can separate us from God's love in Christ.

Once we are joined to Christ Jesus in God's love, there is nothing that can separate us from God. This is true because it is God who made the first move toward us. It is God who desires to love us self-sacrificially, and Jesus demonstrates how that is done. God loves his Son all the way to the cross, and their love is so strong that God raises him from the dead! Being in the love of Christ is as strong as a bear sow which will do anything to protect her cubs. If you want to see how this works, stand in between the sow and her cubs! God's agape love manifested in Jesus protects us from anything that even attempts to get between us and the love of Christ. Like a bear cub grows into an adult bear, we, too, grow from "those who love us in the faith" (Titus 3:15a), that is, from relationships with others, to agape, knowing that we cannot be excommunicated, separated, or cut off from the love of Christ Jesus.

Journal/Meditation: What feeling is engendered in you by your understanding that nothing can separate you from the love of Christ?

Prayer: God, you justify me in your sight with your grace and love. You give me a model of how to respond in faith to your grace and love in your Son, Christ Jesus. Strengthen me in your service as I know that neither hardship, or distress, or persecution, or famine, or nakedness, or peril, or the sword can separate me from the love of Christ through you forever. Amen.

Love Jesus Christ 4

Scripture: ". . . [T]he love of Christ urges us on, because we are convinced that one has died for all; therefore all have died." (2 Cor 5:14)

Reflection: The love of Christ, about which Paul writes in his Second Letter to the Corinthians, is agape. Thus, it is the self-sacrificing love of the dead and risen Christ that drives the focus of the apostle. Jesus demonstrated unconditional love by dying; his example is for those who live so that they may no longer live for themselves but for the Jesus who died and was raised as the Christ by God (2 Cor 5:15). According to Paul, the example of Jesus' agape compels us to a spiritual maturity that engenders the same unimaginable love-always-in-process in us. If agape for us and for God pushed forward Jesus during his life on earth, then the same agape should press us forward not only to participate in Christ's love, but to transform our thinking into a picture of unity. Those of us who are in Christ, according to Paul, are a new creation. The totality of humankind, collectively called the old Adam by Paul, has been recreated into the totality of the new Adam, Christ Jesus, who demonstrated the unimaginable power of self-sacrificial love.

The self-sacrificial love of Christ Jesus urges us to serve as ambassadors. Paul states that God appeals to others through us who are convinced that Jesus died and God raised him from the dead, thus reconciling the whole world to himself through Jesus' act of self-sacrificial love. In other words, through our deeds and words, we demonstrate, like Jesus, that we are spiritually mature with an "undying love for our Lord Jesus Christ" (Eph 6:24). As ambassadors, we represent the paradoxical quality of agape to the world. When the opportunity to steal something presents itself, we do the loving thing and refuse to take it, even though others may walk away with it! When someone is spreading rumors about another, we stop the flow by not passing on what we have heard. When division occurs because of differing opinions, we try to find a way to reconcile the parties, even if it means only agreeing that we disagree! It is the love of Christ that serves as our model and urges us on through death to life.

Journal/Meditation: In what specific ways does the love of Christ urge you to be the best person that you can be? Identify specific situations in which the love of Christ compelled you to be self-sacrificial?

Prayer: God our Father, you graced your Son with self-sacrificial love which compelled him to die for the salvation of the world. Fill me with that same love for you and for him. I ask this through the Lord Jesus Christ, whom you raised from the dead. Amen.

Love of God in Christ Jesus

Scripture: ". . . I am convinced that neither death, nor life, nor angels, nor rulers, nor things present, nor things to come, nor powers, nor height, nor depth, nor anything else in all creation, will be able to separate us from the love of God in Christ Jesus our Lord." (Rom 8:38–39)

Reflection: In his Letter to the Romans, Paul declares that nothing can separate us from the self-sacrificial love of God that is in his anointed One. There are two ways to grasp this love-truth. First, Paul understands Jesus to be one chosen, anointed, by God for a specific purpose. This makes Jesus a conduit, channel, or pipe through whom God's love flows from the Holy One to people. Nothing can break that connection. Also, Paul's concept of the body of Christ underlies his declaration. All those baptized into the death and resurrection of Christ are members of his body. They do what is good for the whole body; individualism disappears. The self-sacrificing love within the community—within the body of Christ—where none is separated is an experience of God's love and, indeed, a conduit of it, in Christ Jesus.

Second, just as two magnets are drawn to each other and cling tightly to each other, so is the power of God's self-sacrificing love to Christ and Christ to us. This is the energy of love. It is unbroken, constant, and powerful. It is so strong that in Christ Jesus it creates a community, a union of all as one body. This is why Paul in his Second Letter to the Corinthians wishes them "[t]he grace of the Lord Jesus Christ, the love of God, and the communion of the Holy Spirit" (2 Cor 13:13). Paul hopes that his readers are filled with God: grace, love, and communion. In other words, just as the Father, Son, and Spirit are one in a communion of love, so are Christians magnetized as one in self-sacrificial love.

Journal/Meditation: Other than the images of conduit and magnets, what metaphor helps you to grasp the truth that nothing can separate you from the love of God in Christ Jesus?

Prayer: Father, neither death, nor life, nor angels, nor rulers, nor things present, nor things to come, nor powers, nor height, nor depth, nor anything else in all creation is able to separate me from your love in Christ Jesus my Lord. All praise be to you—Father, Son, and Holy Spirit—now and forever. Amen.

Love of Jesus Trumps Loving Parents and Children

Scripture: Jesus said, "Whoever loves father or mother more than me is not worthy of me; and whoever loves son or daughter more than me is not worthy of me . . . ." (Matt 10:37)

Reflection: The word for love in the above verse from Matthew's Gospel is philia. Thus, the Matthean Jesus declares that relationship love between a person and his or her father or mother that is greater than one's relationship love with Jesus means that the person is not worthy of Jesus. Parents who love their children relationally more than they love Jesus are also not worthy of Jesus. Thus, in a person's life, all relationships are less important than one's relationship with Jesus. In a culture that boasts of family ties that bind, the Matthean Jesus' declaration about love can be quite upsetting. Responding to the offer of a relationship with Jesus, then, calls for careful discernment, gentle action, and not negative rejection as the author of Luke's Gospel portrays Jesus stating: "Whoever comes to me and does not hate father and mother, wife and children, brothers and sisters, yes, even life itself, cannot be my disciple" (Luke 14:26).

Jesus wants to be on top of everyone's relationship list. This means that family members will have to navigate differences. Parents may have to recognize that a child is called by God in a more intense manner to a ministry of some kind than others are called. Not only can hermits and anchorites or monastics understand their call to be one of separation from the usual cultural norm of husband and wife, children, and grandchildren, but in the past, wars have found brother fighting brother because of their differences in political and religious opinions. When it comes to Jesus, relationship love is not a polite invitation; it is a command to make our relationship with Jesus the most important one on our list. Otherwise, we are not worthy of him.

Journal/Meditation: What deep truth do you discover in Jesus' words about not relating in love to any family member more than Jesus?

Prayer: Ever-living God, your Son taught me that I am not worthy of him if I love spouse, father, mother, children, brothers, or sisters more than him. Fill me with your love that is strong enough to love Jesus first and to love all others as you love them. Amen.

Two Great Commandments: Love God 1

Scripture: "One of the scribes came near . . . , and . . . he asked [Jesus], 'Which commandment is the first of all?' Jesus answered, 'The first is, "Hear, O Israel: the Lord our God, the Lord is one; you shall love the Lord your God with all your heart, and with all your soul, and with all your mind, and with all your strength."'" (Mark 12:28–30)

Reflection: By the time of Jesus, Judaism had moved firmly away from henotheism—the worship of one god as the special god of a specific group of people, while acknowledging or believing in the existence of other gods—to monotheism—the belief that there is only one God. This is illustrated by the Markan Jesus quotation of what is known as the *shema* from the HB (OT) book of Deuteronomy: "Hear, O Israel: The LORD is our God, the LORD alone. You shall love the LORD your God with all your heart, and with all your soul, and with all your might" (Deut 6:4–5). The phrase, "the LORD alone" can also be translated "God is one" or "the LORD is one," as it is in Mark 12:29 above. To the *shema* the Markan Jesus adds that one loves God self-sacrificially with one's mind. In Matthew's version of Jesus' pronouncement, it is a lawyer who asks Jesus about the greatest law (Matt 22:35) to which Jesus replies, "You shall love the Lord your God with all your heart, and with all your soul, and with all your mind" (Matt 22:37). In Luke's version, the lawyer asks Jesus about what he needs to do to inherit eternal life (Luke 10:25). Jesus asks the lawyer what he reads in the law, and the lawyer responds, "You shall love the Lord your God with all your heart, and with all your soul, and with all your strength, and with all your mind . . ." (Luke 10:27). Jesus tells the lawyer that he has given the right answer.

This greatest of commandments is focused on total, self-sacrificial love of the one God. To love God with all our heart is to love with our total being. In Jesus' world, the heart, the focus of attention, represented the seat of intelligence; it was the place where decisions were rendered. To love with all our soul is to love with the very essence that makes each of us unique. The breath of God in us is our personality, our spirit, our life force, our self. To love with all our mind is to love with our intellect, understanding, reason, and worldview. And to love with all our strength is to love with every ability, effort, and power that we have. In other words, Jesus instructs us to love Being (God) with our total being (personhood). With our total presence we love self-sacrificially the Presence; we come before the one God with our totality to self-sacrifice it exclusively, unconditionally, and timelessly.

Journal/Meditation: How do you love Being (God) with the totality of your being—heart, soul, mind, and strength?

Prayer: O LORD, my God, you are one. Grant that I may love you with all my heart, with all my soul, with all my mind, and with all my strength. I ask this through Jesus Christ now and forever. Amen.

Two Great Commandments: Love God 2

Scripture: Jesus said, "No one can serve two masters; for a slave will either hate the one and love the other, or be devoted to the one and despise the other. You cannot serve God and wealth." (Matt 6:24)

Reflection: The self-sacrificial love illustrated by the author of Matthew's Gospel in the above verse illustrates what ought to be our ultimate concern, our fundamental option, when it comes to serving and loving God. The author of Luke's Gospel is even more direct, accusing the Pharisees of being concerned more about tithes than about justice and the love of God (Luke 11:42). Luke, like Matthew, also records Jesus stating, "No slave can serve two masters; for a slave will either hate the one and love the other, or be devoted to the one and despise the other. You cannot serve God and wealth" (Luke 16:13). In other words, you are who you hang out with! If you discover that you spend more time being ultimately concerned about wealth—cash, house, car, etc.—then that is where your heart is. If you discover that you spend more time fundamentally focused on God, then you are cultivating a relationship with the Divine.

For those of us living in a capitalistic culture, this may not be easy to navigate, especially when money, buying and selling stock, and net worth are ever before our eyes. What capitalism fails to notice is that the God who created all also owns all. Thus, from a biblical point of view owning wealth or laying claim to it is not possible. In other words, ownership of anything is an illusion; all is on loan to us. All we can do is to serve the real owner: God. To approach this from a different perspective, we cannot be in the presence of wealth and the Divine Presence at the same time and give both our undivided attention. Both the Matthean and the

Lukan Jesus state that we are to exist for God alone, that we are to base our being on Being, that we serve infinite Love that gives itself away in creation and its self-sacrificial evolution.

Journal/Meditation: Do you live under the illusion of ownership? How does that illusion change you? How could becoming aware of this illusion draw you deeper into self-sacrificing love?

Prayer: Lord GOD, your Son has taught me that I cannot serve you and wealth. Fill me with the grace of love and devotion to you alone through Jesus Christ, who lives and reigns with you and the Holy Spirit, one God, forever and ever. Amen.

Two Great Commandments: Love God 3

Scripture: "We know that all things work together for good for those who love God, who are called according to his purpose." (Rom 8:28)

Reflection: Paul's simple statement about self-sacrificial love is loaded with potential reflection. First, Paul understands that "the God of love" (2 Cor 13:11) possesses a universal plan. And that plan or purpose unfolds in the lives of those who love God. In Pauline thought, Abraham is the incarnation of part of God's plan; God declares him righteous or graced. The plan continues in Moses' flesh; God gives him the Torah to guide his people. The plan culminates in Jesus, who, through his life, death, and resurrection re-creates the human race in such a way that it can receive "the love of God" (2 Cor 13:13) as the LORD intends. According to Paul, all things created by God work together and toward the realization of God's plan for those who self-sacrificially love God and respond to his call to participate in his purpose.

If Paul were around today, two thousand years later, he would say that the divine plan has continued for another two-thousand years. God continues to offer his self-sacrificing love to people, who can accept it and respond with the same love. Reflection raises our awareness or consciousness about the part we have been called to play in God's plan. Everyone who loves God has some small role. And that little piece is validated by our daily experiences of the flow of divine self-sacrificial energy—love—that fills our lives. By being attentive to them, we come to see evermore clearly God's purpose for our lives, that is, what we need to be about as we are being drawn deeper and deeper into sacrificial love. Once we answer Love's call, we are predestined to be shaped and guided in a direction that continues to unfold God's purpose.

Journal/Meditation: What has been your role in God's plan in the past? What do you discern God's plan is for you right now?

Prayer: "O the depth of the riches and wisdom and knowledge of God! How unsearchable are his judgments and how inscrutable his ways! For from him and through him and to him are all things. To him be glory forever. Amen." (Rom 11:33, 36)

Two Great Commandments: Love God 4

Scripture: "Listen, my beloved brothers and sisters. Has not God chosen the poor in the world to be rich in faith and to be heirs of the kingdom that he has promised to those who love him?" (Jas 2:5)

Reflection: According to the author of the Letter of James, those who love God have been promised the kingdom. Earlier, James states, "Blessed is anyone who endures temptation. Such a one has stood the test and will receive the crown of life that the Lord has promised to those who love him" (Jas 1:12). James advocates self-sacrificial love in action; this is hard love. It is not easy to love God even when a promise is involved. The author of this letter presumes that there is a reward for good deeds done, such as serving the poor and enduring temptation. We might refer to this today as the heavenly bank account system. Love is demonstrated with works; those who love God self-sacrificially demonstrate their faith with their works. Of course, Paul would object to this approach since he believed faith alone was enough, but he was long dead by the time James wrote this letter!

Agape love needs to be as strong as a ship's rudder; otherwise, even with the promises that James attaches to it, it will fail. Even Jesus' disciples falter when crossing the sea or lake (of Galilee) (Mark

4:35–41; Matt 8:18, 23–27; Luke 8:22–25). Jesus is asleep in trust of God in the midst of a windstorm. The disciples fear that they will perish, so they wake Jesus, who calms the sea or lake. Self-sacrificial love is not easy when storms arise. As James indicates, we live into self-sacrificial love—and spiritual growth—when we do not give into temptation and when we serve the poor. With a strong love-rudder we remain rich in faith that prompts us to do good works, trusting that God is faithful to his promise of eternal life in his kingdom.

Journal/Meditation: What trials have you endured with good works? What poor have you met with good works?

Prayer: LORD God, you have promised the crown of life to those who love you and demonstrate it through their good works. Make me rich in faith that I may be an heir of your kingdom, where you live and reign with Jesus Christ and the Holy Spirit, one God, forever and ever. Amen.

Two Great Commandments: Love Neighbor 1

Scripture: A lawyer answered Jesus, "'You shall love the Lord your God with all your heart, and with all your soul, and with all your strength, and with all your mind; and you neighbor as yourself.' And [Jesus] said to him, 'You have given the right answer; do this, and you will live.'" (Luke 10:27–28)

Reflection: Only in Luke's Gospel is the love of God, the love of neighbor, and the love of self one statement that is made by a lawyer and affirmed by Jesus. In Mark's Gospel, after a scribe asks Jesus about the greatest commandment, Jesus tells him to love God with all his soul, mind, and strength. Then the Markan Jesus states, "The second [greatest commandment] is this, 'You shall love you neighbor as yourself'" (Mark 12:31, 33). In Matthew's Gospel, as in Luke's, it is a lawyer who asks Jesus which is the greatest commandment to which Jesus responds by telling him to love God with his whole heart, soul, and mind. Then, he adds, "And a second [commandment] is like it: 'You shall love your neighbor as yourself.'" (Matt 22:39). The author of Matthew's Gospel had already established the love of neighbor as one loves self (Matt 19:19) going so far as to present Jesus declaring in the sermon on the mount, "You have heard that it was said, 'You shall love your neighbor and hate your enemy.' But I say to you, Love your enemies and pray for those who persecute you" (Matt 5:43–44). Thus, self-sacrificial love is extended to enemies and persecutors. This is best represented by Luke's unique parable of the Samaritan (enemy of the Jews), who loved and helped the Jewish man (enemy of the Samaritans) in the ditch (Luke 10:29–37).

In all three settings and versions of the statement about love of neighbor, the comparison begins with love of self, that is, self-sacrificial love of self. This love is a willingness to love self to such a degree that it overflows outward. If it only flowed inward, then it would be narcissism. This is not emotional love; this is objective love. We decide to love others, to trust them, to respect them and their dignity and concerns, to put their interests and safety on a level with and maybe above our own. This is the agape that is able to love enemies, who are neighbors. The love of neighbor as we love ourselves grounds us and allows us to experience God. From love itself—God—flows love of self outward to love of neighbor, who may be an enemy. This gives us the ability to see the Divine Presence in our uniquely created self and in the uniquely created self of one labeled persecutor. Thus, self-sacrificial love overcomes division between one and his or her enemy and makes us one, just like the love of God makes us one with the God who loves us first. In other words, love of the opposition is best demonstrated by Jesus, who went willingly to the cross, where he loved and forgave his enemies before he died (Luke 23:34). To put it another way, self-sacrificial love is like a mustard seed that grows and grows and cannot be contained; it becomes so huge that it can encompass even enemies.

Journal/Meditation: In what specific ways do you love your neighbors as you love yourself? In what specific ways do you love your enemies?

Prayer: Father in heaven, you make your sun rise on the good and the evil, and you send rain on the righteous and on the unrighteous. Make me perfect in sacrificial love that I may be like you forever and ever. Amen.

Two Great Commandments: Love Neighbor 2

Scripture: ". . . [T]he whole law is summed up on a single commandment, 'You shall love your neighbor as yourself.'" (Gal 5:14)

Reflection: The love of neighbor as one loves oneself in Pauline thought is a summary of the six hundred thirteen precepts of Torah (Law). Besides the emphasis of it in the Letter to the Galatians, Paul also declares in his Letter to the Romans that all commandments are summarized in this word: "'Love your neighbor as yourself.' Love does no wrong to a neighbor; therefore, love is the fulfilling of the law" (Rom 13:9–10). Even Paul's nemesis, James, tells his readers, "You do well if you really fulfill the royal law according to the scripture, 'You shall love your neighbor as yourself'" (Jas 2:8). Torah states, ". . . [Y]ou shall love your neighbor as yourself: I am the LORD" (Lev 19:18). However, this love of neighbor defines neighbor as a fellow Israelite. When Jesus, Paul, and James teach love of neighbor, they expand the Torah to include all people. Thus to have the same self-sacrificial love for our neighbors as we have for ourselves may seem contradictory or paradoxical at first, but the truth is discovered by going deeper.

The big picture of self-sacrificial love helps us to understand that all of us are equal. All we owe in our unanimity is love. This agape love is what distinguishes Christians from others and at the same time unites them to all. Love pulls us out of ourselves; love calls. Love pulls God out of himself; love is incarnate in Jesus. Self-sacrificial love began a world-changing event. Jesus did God's will in love. Our love of neighbor as we love ourselves is God's goal for us from the beginning. This makes God a mystery of love and relationship. This is why Paul can declare that all of the precepts of Torah are summed up and fulfilled by the love of neighbor as we love ourselves. Authentic love of neighbor represents spiritual maturity; it is the ability to open our arms and receive all people into our circle of love with respect and dignity, much like Pope Francis does wherever he goes. The love of neighbor guides us to where we need to be in the ongoing process of loving more and more until we reach the source of love: the Divine Presence. That is why the whole Law is fulfilled by self-sacrificial love. St. Augustine may have put this more succinctly when he wrote that people should love and do what they want. Augustine understood that the love of neighbor encompasses and fulfills any other commandments. A person who loves his or her neighbor the way he or she loves himself or herself will never do any harm to the neighbor. Why? Because it is impossible to love self-sacrificially and do harm to others.

Journal/Meditation: In what specific situation have you reached a depth of self-sacrificial love of neighbor that fulfills all the commandments?

Prayer: LORD, all of your commandments of the past are summed up in the new commandment to love my neighbor as I love myself. With the gift of your Spirit, help me live the love that does no wrong to my neighbor as the fulfillment of your law. I ask this in the name of Jesus, who is Lord forever and ever. Amen.

3

Love, God, Son, and Others

Love One Another 1

Scripture: "No one has ever seen God; if we love one another, God lives in us, and his love is perfected in us." (1 John 4:12)

    Reflection: The author of the letters of John presumes that no one has ever seen God, because God is invisible. No one can, literally, touch, taste, smell, hear, or see the Divine. By loving one another, we lift the veil on the invisible by loving the other who is visible. As First John puts it, ". . . [T]his is the message you have heard from the beginning, that we should love one another" (1 John 3:11; cf. 2 John 1:5). The author specifies the message that has been heard, stating, "And this is his commandment, that we should believe in the name of his Son Jesus Christ and love one another, just as he has commanded us" (1 John 3:23). Even more direct is the command given by Jesus in John's Gospel: "I give you a new commandment, that you love one another. Just as I have loved you, you also should love one another" (John 13:34; 15:12, 17). The First Letter of John explains that we "love one another, because love is from God; everyone who loves is born of God and knows

God" (1 John 4:7). Therefore, "since God loves us so much, we also ought to love one another" (1 John 4:11).

According to Jesus in John's Gospel, "By this everyone will know that you are my disciples, if you have love for one another" (John 13:35). Thus, there is a broader, a more universal movement, to self-sacrificing love that moves even beyond one's neighbor. We may call it discipleship love; it forms a bridge from God through Jesus and through the church to the community. In other words, God loves Jesus and sent him from heaven to earth as a demonstration of his love. Jesus loves those he calls to follow him. Those followers love one another because all love comes from God through Jesus, and the love of one another unites the whole world in self-sacrificial love. God loves himself through those who love one another, just as Jesus demonstrated. God calls us through our love for one another to connect our love energy to God's so that there is but one heart (Jesus) pumping love-blood through all the veins and arteries of those who love one another connecting all to One.

Journal/Reflection: In what specific ways have you seen God by loving others?

Prayer: No one has ever seen you, God, but if I love others, you live in me, and your love is perfected in me. Grant me a deeper self-sacrificial love that I may keep the commandment of your Son, Jesus Christ, who is Lord forever and ever. Amen.

Love One Another 2

Scripture: "Owe no one anything, except to love one another; for the one who loves another has fulfilled the law." (Rom 13:8)

Reflection: Most of us do not recognize the radicalism of Paul's statement in his Letter to the Romans. The person who loves self-sacrificially has fulfilled the Torah, according to Paul, all six hundred thirteen precepts! That is quite a statement for a Pharisee, that is, one trained in Torah, to make! In his Letter to the Galatians, the apostle approaches agape love from the point of view of freedom and slavery. He writes, ". . . [Y]ou were called to freedom, brothers and sisters; only do not use your freedom as an opportunity for self-indulgence, but through love become slaves to one another" (Gal 5:13). He goes on to say that the whole law is summed up in the single commandment to love one's neighbor as one loves himself or herself. Picking up on this Pauline concept, the author of the Letter to the Ephesians urges his readers "with all humility and gentleness, with patience, [to bear] with one another in love" (Eph 4:2). Likewise, the author of the Second Letter to the Thessalonians remarks that the "love of everyone . . . for one another is increasing" among the members of the community in Thessalonica (2 Thess 1:3).

What we notice in these biblical remarks is that self-sacrificial love spills over into love for one another and is an ongoing process. There is no end point, because it is a process of growth in transcending differences to the point where the differences no longer matter. Some might call this kind of love tolerant. No matter how we refer to it, divisions cease as we love another as he or she is because love is Love! Its idealist goal, according to Paul in his Letter to the Galatians, is for lovers to be slaves to one another, to see that loving one another is, in fact, loving one's self and God. Self-sacrificial love is able to see the beautiful differences in others and love them, appreciating the un-likenesses of others just like the likenesses. Such love slavery is not bondage. Paradoxically, loving without divisions is freedom to appreciate (even love) differences while acknowledging them. Thus, love unites body and spirit; love is the key to peace for the self; and love of one another creates joy in unimaginable ways.

Journal/Meditation: How have you paid the debt to love others? How have you experienced love slavery as freedom?

Prayer: Heavenly Father, your Son taught me to owe nothing except love to you, to others, and to myself. Bathe me in your divine love that creates unity out of division and unites all people in a song of praise of you, Father, Son, and Holy Spirit, forever and ever. Amen.

Love One Another 3

Scripture: ". . . [L]et us consider how to provoke one another to love and good deeds." (Heb 10:24)

Reflection: "To provoke" means to elicit a response, to cause a deed or activity, to stir someone to action, to incite another. Coming from the Latin verb *voco*, meaning *to call*, the word implies calling another to respond to love. Yes, we can provoke one another in many negative ways, and that seems to be the usual way we employ the verb. So, two people in conversation can provoke anger if they disagree vehemently. Newspaper stories often provoke letters from readers, and almost everyone is familiar with all the provoking that takes place on social media. Nevertheless, the author of Hebrews urges his readers to provoke one another to love. The First Letter of Peter, likewise, urges "genuine mutual love, lov[ing] one another deeply from the heart" (1 Pet 1:22). Later in the same letter, the author writes, "Above all, maintain constant love for one another, for love covers a multitude of sins" (1 Pet 4:8). In other words, genuine, self-sacrificial love forgives by removing judgment.

How much would the world change if we provoked love instead of war, killing, boundary disputes, angry words, hate, etc.? How much would the world change if we provoked love instead of politics, creeds, races, sex, etc.? Instead of claiming that our lives are about us, if we provoked the love that brings us into existence and keeps us there, we would quickly recognize that our lives are not our own in the individualistic, competitive, consumer culture in which we live. The universal picture of self-sacrificial love reminds us that when we love one another, we love God. And when we love God, we love God's world and all who are in it. And that love, hopefully, provokes one another to love. In other words, we love God by provoking one another to love. Provoked love engenders fellowship, community, and identity, which further stirs love and good deeds. Fellowship among lovers recharges all with spiritual life, levity, positive encouragement, accountability, and truth and honesty. That is why the author of the First Letter of Peter tells his readers, "Greet one another with a kiss of love" (1 Pet 5:14a).

Journal/Meditation: In whom have you recently provoked love? How did that occur?

Prayer: Through the incarnation of your Son, O LORD, you provoked love in our world. Through your Spirit, help me consider how to provoke others to love and good deeds. I ask this in the name of Jesus now and forever. Amen.

Brotherly/Sisterly Love 1

Scripture: "Let love be genuine; hate what is evil, hold fast to what is good; love one another with mutual affection; outdo one another in showing honor." (Rom 12:9–10)

Reflection: Paul's exhortation in his Letter to the Romans about letting love be genuine is friendship or brotherly/sisterly love, philia. The apostle explains this type of love as mutual affection. The author of the Letter to the Hebrews echoes Paul's sentiment writing, "Let mutual love continue" (Heb 13:1). The Second Letter of Peter exhorts its readers to support "godliness with mutual affection, and mutual affection with love" (2 Pet 1:7), while Paul's First Letter to the Thessalonians records that agape, self-sacrificial "love of the brothers and sisters," is occurring in the community because the Thessalonians "have been taught by God to love one another" affectionately as brothers and sisters (1 Thess 1:9). Thus, some of the writers of the books of the CB (NT) view mutual affection as a tendency within the Christian community, what today might be called a friendly feeling of tenderness or fondness.

Friendship love—brotherly or sisterly love—springs out of genuine care, genuine concern for the well being of others in one's circle of friends and in the community of believers. It is the type of love that supports those we count on and supports those who count on us. It is a realization that the divine energy of God—love—flows through us. Brotherly or sisterly love implies that the cause is bigger than I; there is camaraderie among Christians, an experience of belonging, being in a group together, and all of it flowing from

35

and back to God. Common affection, honor, esteem for brothers and sisters is limitless because the source, God, is limitless. Philia creates the space where we can be ourselves unapologetically. The centrifugal force of love flows out of the Trinity, and its centripetal force draws us into God. When we demonstrate brotherly/sisterly love, we become the mediators or conduits of Divine Love. It is as simple as showing respect to or appreciation for another while being in his or her presence.

Journal/Meditation: Recently, how have you loved another with mutual affection? How have you outdone yourself in showing honor to another?

Prayer: Almighty God, you have taught me to love others with mutual affection and honor. Fill me with your Spirit of love that I may show genuine love to all my brothers and sisters in the various communities to which I belong. Grant this through Jesus Christ my Lord. Amen.

Brotherly/Sisterly Love 2

Scripture: "Those who say, 'I love God,' and hate their brothers or sisters, are liars; for those who do not love a brother or sister whom they have seen, cannot love God whom they have not seen." (1 John 4:20)

Reflection: The author of the First Letter of John presents a dualistic approach to self-sacrificial love within the community. One point of his dualism represents those who love God and hate members in the community. The other point of his dualism represents those who love God and love the brothers and sisters in the community. The author declares those who fall under his first point to be liars. Earlier in the letter, the author had this to say: "The children of God and the children of the devil are revealed in this way: all who do not do what is right are not from God, nor are those who do not love their brothers and sisters" (1 John 3:10). Doing what is right involves the use of the world's goods for brothers and sisters in need (1 John 3:17). Or, as indicated above, you cannot love the unseen God if you do not love your visible brothers and sisters. The author of the First Letter of Peter puts it this way: "Honor everyone. Love the family of believers. Fear God" (1 Pet 2:17abc).

The visible brothers and sisters manifest the invisible God. Furthermore, love is not visible; it cannot be measured by the cup! But love can be manifested by meeting the needs of brothers and sisters. Thus, a person cannot hate the visible brothers and sisters in the community and claim to love the God who loves them. Self-sacrificial love of the brothers and sisters reveals or makes visible the love of God. According to the First Letter of John, self-sacrificial love is an obligation. We see brothers and sisters in need and put their need above our own needs, desires, time, etc. This may involve housing, food, clothing, etc. Whatever love we show to the brothers and sisters in need reveals that we abide in God's love. Otherwise, we are liars; otherwise, we are children of the devil, and we are not loving the family of believers.

Journal/Meditation: In what specific ways do you reveal the invisible God by your love of visible brothers and sisters?

Prayer: Keep my love for you genuine, heavenly Father. Through my good works for the brothers and sisters I can see, reveal your presence in the world. May I always abide in the love you share with your Son, Jesus Christ, and the Holy Spirit, forever and ever. Amen.

Love Friends

Scripture: ". . . [T]he sisters [Mary and Martha] sent a message to Jesus, 'Lord, he whom you love is ill.'" (John 11:3)

Reflection: In the forty-four-verse Johannine account of Jesus raising Lazarus from the dead, the message sent by Lazarus's two sisters refers to Jesus' love for their brother as friendship. However, two verses later in the story, the author states that "Jesus loved Martha and her sister [Mary] and Lazarus" self-sacrificially (John 11:5). These two statements prepare for Jesus' reflection on sacrificial love four chapters later in John's Gospel when he states: "No one has greater love than this, to lay down one's life for one's friends" (John 15:13). It is self-sacrificial love that Jesus demands of his friends. "As the Father has loved me," he tells them, "so I have loved you; abide in my love" (John 15:9). It is this mutual abiding-in—Father in Son, Son in Father, Friends in Son, and Son in Friends—which makes Jesus' friends mediators of self-sacrificial love from God through Jesus to others and from others to God through Jesus. The self-sacrificial love that comes from God compels us to love our friends.

Love unlocks a world of spiritual power among friends. It creates a community of those who are willing to lay down their lives. Such a foundation is not a decision made because God loves us first and brings us into existence, but because we respond to the Divine Love and abide in it. Self-sacrificial love is our destiny; remaining in love implies that the process of always becoming a more loving person in mind, body, heart, and soul has no end. According to John's Gospel, Jesus loved Lazarus as a friend, but he also loved Lazarus, Martha, and Mary self-sacrificially through his encounter with them. The love that comes from God is like an overflowing fountain, which invites all to come and drink and to abide. Jesus drinks of God's love and summons us to drink of God's love through him. Love's engagement with others preserves life, leads to knowledge of others, destabilizes both the lover and the loved, begins with a genuine encounter, and raises the dead! When friends accept and act in accordance with agape love, they remain steadfast and faithful to each other.

Journal/Meditation: What friends do you love self-sacrificially? What spiritual power does that love unlock for you and them?

Prayer: Father, as you have loved your Son, Jesus has loved me self-sacrificially, demonstrating that no one has greater love than the person who lays down his or her life for his or her friends. Through the Holy Spirit, keep me abiding in this powerful and sacred love now and forever. Amen.

Love Enemies

Scripture: Jesus spoke, "You have heard that it was said, 'You shall love your neighbor and hate your enemy.' But I say to you, Love your enemies and pray for those who persecute you . . . . For if you love those who love you, what reward do you have?" (Matt 5:43–44, 46a)

Reflection: Love knows no boundaries, not even toward one's enemies. This may be the most difficult form of love to accept, yet the most fruitful in practice. Jesus clearly states that we are to love our enemies (Luke 6:27), to pray for our enemies (Luke 6:28), and to do good to those who hate us (Luke 6:27). As in Matthew's Gospel, so in Luke's Gospel, Jesus asks, "If you love those who love you, what credit is that to you? If you do good to those who do good to you, what credit is that to you? (Luke 6:32a, 33a) However, Jesus never tells us what happens when we love our enemies. What is the reward that Jesus mentions in Matthew's Gospel and in Luke's Gospel (6:35b)?

Jesus created what we will refer to as a common denominator. This means that Jesus made a point to bring everyone to the same level of being. Rich, poor, priest, or slave, Jesus treated each individual the same, even his enemies. Jesus spoke about self-sacrificial love for all. Living under the rule of the Roman Empire with its various social levels—where peasant was near the bottom of the list—and the practice of social domination known as crucifixion, it would be extremely easy to see Roman soldiers performing terrible crimes and immediately dehumanize them for their actions. However, the common denominator according to Jesus is that no matter how people are labeled—friends or enemies—all are human beings; all are children of the Father in heaven (Matt 6:45) or children of the Most High (Luke 6:35). While it is extremely easy to see the world dualistically (in black and white, good and bad, friend and enemy), Jesus teaches us to see the world as God does in a radical new light. The reward for loving our enemies is immersion into a life experience that brings out the best in each and every one of us; it offers hope for humanity even in the worst of times, and it allows us to live our life to its full potential.

Journal/Meditation: When have you most recently loved an enemy? How did it feel? What reward did you receive?

Prayer: Most High God, change me, mold me, and form me into one of your dearest children. Father, help me to love my enemies and to do good to those who hate me. Hear this prayer for all my enemies through Jesus Christ, your Son, who is Lord forever and ever. Amen.

Love Saints and Believers

Scripture: "I pray that you may have the power to comprehend, with all the saints, what is the breadth and length and height and depth, and to know the love of Christ that surpasses knowledge, so that you may be filled with all the fullness of God." (Eph 3:18–19)

Reflection: "I have heard of your faith in the Lord Jesus and your love toward all the saints," states the author of the Letter to the Ephesians (1:15). The author of the Letter to the Colossians echoes this sentiment, writing that he has heard of their "faith in Christ Jesus and of the love that [they] have for all the saints" (Col 1:4). Likewise, the author of the Letter to the Hebrews assures his readers that God will not overlook their work "and the love that [they] showed for his sake in serving the saints" (Heb 6:10). All three authors refer to members of the community of believers as saints. This is not the commonly accepted notion of today which uses the term to refer to those men and women who have been added to the list (canonized) of those members of the community who have been declared to have a privileged place in heaven and are worthy of imitation and veneration. All three CB (NT) authors are acknowledging the self-sacrificial love of members of the Christian community shown to each other.

The second-generation Pauline author of the Letter to the Ephesians prays that his readers will know the breadth—the distance from side to side, the length—the distance from end to end, the height—the distance from the lowest point to the highest point, and the depth—the distance from top to bottom, and to know the love of Christ that surpasses knowledge, so that they may be filled with all the fullness of God. Self-sacrificial love is all-encompassing, amazing, endless, and perfect in Christ Jesus. It is universal. If you were to draw a box so big that you cannot see its lines from side to side, from end to end, from lowest to highest, from top to bottom, that is the world of self-sacrificial love that the author of Ephesians wishes for his community; love is a universal language. When this corporate self-sacrificial love community is viewed by others, they want to be a part of it; they want to be incorporated into it. However, in today's world the infinite love box may be seen as exclusive, a Christian clique or a gated community. Our task is never to let that happen by loving all the saints without limit, reserve, or judgment.

Journal/Meditation: How do you make the community of saints and believers more welcoming, that is, more universal, so that more people participate in the fullness of God?

Prayer: I pray, Father, that you give me the power to comprehend, with all the saints, what is the breadth and length and height and depth, and to know the love of Christ that surpasses knowledge, so that I may be filled with all your fullness now and forever. Amen.

Love the Body

Scripture: ". . . [S]peaking the truth in love, we must grow up in every way into him who is the head, into Christ, from whom the whole body, joined and knit together by every ligament with which it is equipped, as each part is working properly, promotes the body's growth in building itself up in love." (Eph 4:15–16)

Reflection: For the author of the Letter to the Ephesians, self-sacrificial or agape love is not only the basis for speaking the truth within the community of believers, but it is simultaneously the vehicle for growing the community of believers. Without a heart, liver, or brain, your individual body cannot function; if you are missing a vital organ, the body will die. Self-sacrificial love within the body of believers enables members to be vital groups, like organs or veins, that work together to accomplish the common good of the whole. We love and care for the body of Christ, just as we exercise our physical bodies to foster health and longevity.

The second-generation Pauline author of the Letter to the Ephesians elaborates on Paul's metaphor of the body of Christ by naming Christ as head of the body. In his Letter to the Romans, Paul does not write about their being a head of the body: "For as in one body we have many members, and not all the members have the same function, so we, who are many, are one body in Christ, and individually we are members one of another" (Rom 12:4–5). The apostle further elaborates on this in his First Letter to the Corinthians (12:12–31) in which he states that each person's individual body with its many members is a model for the one body of Christ. Like the author of the Letter to the Ephesians does, the author of the Letter to the Colossians also makes his own application of the Pauline metaphor by stating that the body of Christ is the church (Col 1:24). According to Ephesians, the head of the body is the model for all the members of the body. Thus, we are responsible for promoting the whole body's growth self-sacrificially. When all the parts are jointed together and work properly, the body grows in alignment with its head, Christ. The most fruitful way to achieve this is through self-sacrificial love.

Journal/Meditation: In what specific ways does your self-sacrificial love promote the growth of your Christian community into Christ?

Prayer: Mighty God, you have spoken your truth in love to me through your Son, Jesus Christ, the head of the body of believers. Through the Holy Spirit, knit me ever more closely to him and equip me to promote the body's growth into the head of the church, Jesus Christ, who is Lord forever and ever. Amen.

Husbands Love Wives/Wives Love Husbands

Scripture: "Husbands, love your wives, just as Christ loved the church and gave himself up for her, in order to make her holy by cleansing her with the washing of water by the word, so as to present the church to himself in splendor, without a spot or wrinkle or anything of the kind—yes, so that she may be holy and without blemish. In the same way, husbands should love their wives as they do their own bodies. He who loves his wife loves himself. For no one ever hates his own body, but he nourishes and tenderly cares for it, just as Christ does for the church, because we are members of his body. 'For this reason a man will leave his father and mother and be joined to his wife, and the two will become one flesh.' This is a great mystery, and I am applying it to Christ and the church. Each of you, however, should love his wife as himself, and a wife should respect her husband." (Eph 5:25–33)

Reflection: In the above reflection from the author of the Letter to the Ephesians, we find radical words, which do not carry the same punch as they did two-thousand years ago. In an unequal, patriarchal culture infused with honor for men and shame for women, they are anti-cultural words. In a patriarchal culture, a man either bought his wife (dowry) or her father paid him to take her! A wife was considered a man's personal property! Honor could be given only to men; shame could be attributed only to women. In Ephesians, husbands are told to love their wives self-sacrificially, that is, in the same way that they love themselves—not hating their own bodies, but nourishing and tenderly caring for them. Likewise, wives should display the same respect and self-sacrificial love for their husbands. Furthermore, the author of the Letter to the Colossians tells husbands to love their wives and never to treat them harshly (Col 3:19) to further emphasize the radical change in perspective that is occurring in the Christian community. While the Letter to Titus uses philia, the author, nevertheless, records the shift that is taking place in the culture, when he tells older women to encourage young women to love their husbands and to love their children (Titus 2:4).

The primary focus of the passage from Ephesians, however, is on the parallel the author wants to present between the self-sacrificial love that should exist between a husband and wife and Christ and the church. The author wants his readers to put into practice

Jesus' teaching about loving others as one loves one's self, since all are members of Christ's body. The love of husband and wife—the mystery of two becoming one—is applied to Christ, the husband or bridegroom, and to the church, the wife or bride. The author presents the church, the community of believers, as the highest priority, the center of attention, the navel of life. Just as the husband is the center of attention for his wife, and just as the wife is the center of attention for her husband, Ephesians wants all believers—wives—to be focused on the church—the husband— Christ, who sacrificed himself for her holiness. In that way, husbands and wives, who experience the mystery of two becoming one, reflect the mystery of Christ and the church, also two becoming one.

Journal/Meditation: If you are married, how do you and your spouse reflect the mystery of Christ and the church? If you are not married, how do you and your closest friends reflect the mystery of Christ and the church?

Prayer: Heavenly Father, your Son, Jesus Christ, gave himself for the church to make her holy and present her to you in splendor. Guide all husbands and wives into deeper unity that they may reflect the sacrificial love of Christ and reveal its great mystery to all. I ask this through the same Jesus Christ my Lord. Amen.

Paul's Love for Corinthians

Scripture: "Now as you excel in everything, in utmost eagerness, and in our love for you—so we want you to excel also in this generous undertaking." (2 Cor 8:7)

Reflection: Paul is often thought of as a sword-carrying, gruff letter-writer who, after attempting to destroy Christianity after its birth, became its representative to Jews and, primarily, to Gentiles. The "generous undertaking" referred to in the above passage is a collection in which he desires the Corinthian community to participate. However, the focus here is not on gathering funds; in this letter, Paul presents himself as loving the Corinthians self-sacrificially, much the same way parents love their children by willing to do anything for them. In other words, Paul wants to give himself away to the Corinthians. "I will most gladly spend and be spent for you," he writes. "If I love you more, am I to be loved less?" (2 Cor 12:15) Earlier in the letter he had told them that he wanted to let them know the abundant love that he has for them (2 Cor 2:4). In fact, he boasts about them to others because he loves them (2 Cor 11:11).

After reading the apostle's words in Second Corinthians, we cannot help but be touched by his tenderness. In the truest sense of the word, this is one of Paul's love letters. Like any other love-letter writer, Paul gives himself away to those he loves. He has invested some of his life in the Corinthians, even when they have some problems in their community. While he may be anguishing or heartbroken, he loves them nevertheless. He wants them to keep growing stronger while he corrects some of their behavior and, at the same time, reminds them how dear they are to him.

Journal/Meditation: In what specific way have you indicated your love for another, such as a love-letter, a love-card, a love-e-mail, a love-text, etc.? What tenderness did you convey?

Prayer: In whatever I excel, Father, it is because of your love for me. Grant me the grace of utmost eagerness in faith and the love of the Spirit through Jesus Christ, my Lord. Amen.

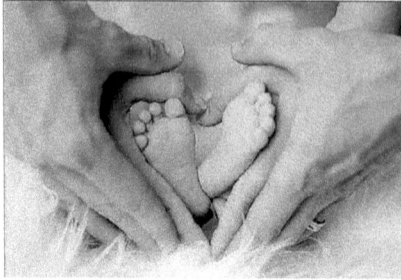

4

Beloved

Beloved at Baptism

Scripture: ". . . [A] voice came from heaven, 'You are my Son, the Beloved; with you I am well pleased.'" (Mark 1:11)

Reflection: Each of the three narratives about Jesus' baptism differs one from another. For example, in Mark's Gospel, only Jesus hears the voice from heaven identifying him as a Beloved Son. In Matthew's Gospel, John the Baptist hears the voice along with Jesus (Matt 3:17); in Luke's Gospel, all the people hear the voice (Luke 3:22). In Greek, the word *beloved* is formed from *agape*, self-sacrificial love. Thus, when the voice from heaven identifies Jesus as beloved, the Father indicates that he sacrifices himself in the Son, and the Son sacrifices himself on the cross. In this, the Father is well pleased. The second-generation, Pauline-flavored letters of Ephesians and Colossians also refer to God's pleasure taken in his "glorious grace that he freely bestowed on us in the Beloved" (Eph 1:6) after transferring us "into the kingdom of his beloved Son" (Col 1:13).

The words of the voice from heaven are a blending of Psalm 2:7 and Isaiah 42:1, probably done first by the author of Mark's

Gospel and copied by both the author of Matthew's Gospel and Luke's Gospel. Naming Jesus beloved identifies him as one loved very much, adored, cherished, treasured, and precious—more than Judean kings at their coronation. Such self-sacrificial beloved status becomes the basis for the gospels' teaching about Jesus' proclamation of the Father's kingdom and the love of God and the love of others as one loves one's self. The torn-apart heavens at Jesus' baptism indicate that God, who lived above the heavens, has come to earth in the person of a beloved Son and initiated a new way of living in the new kingdom. After being transferred to this kingdom, we are named beloved by God; we sacrifice ourselves in love from the day of birth to the day of death, and in this new way of life, the Father is well pleased.

Journal/Meditation: How are you a beloved one, loved very much, adored, cherished, treasured, and precious?

Prayer: Father, you have freely bestowed your glorious grace upon me in your Beloved Son. With your Holy Spirit guide me through his kingdom in this life that I may enjoy it forever in the next. Hear this prayer in the name of Jesus the Lord. Amen.

Beloved at Transfiguration

Scripture: ". . . [F]rom the cloud came a voice that said, 'This is my Son, my Chosen; listen to him!'" (Luke 9:35)

Reflection: Like the declaration of Jesus' beloved status at his baptism, there is the announcement of his beloved status at his transfiguration—except for Luke's Gospel! The author of Mark's Gospel narrates his transfiguration story in such a manner to echo the voice at the baptism (Mark 9:7). Just as the voice at the baptism launched the proclamation of the kingdom of God, so the voice at the transfiguration launches the proclamation of the death and resurrection of Jesus. The author of Matthew's Gospel doesn't understand the connection Mark was making and keeps the story pretty much intact (Matt 17:5). Likewise, when the author of Second Peter narrates the event, he maintains the beloved status of the Son in whom the Father is well pleased (2 Pet 1:17). However, with his theme of being chosen by God, the author of Luke's Gospel presents the voice from the cloud (a clear reference to God's presence as cloud to the Israelites in their desert wanderings and in the Jerusalem Temple) as picking Jesus for the mission to Jews and Gentiles alike.

To be beloved or chosen is to be son. The metaphor of a divine Father-Son relationship is based on human father-son relationships. In other words, we don't have language to describe how God and Jesus are related; so, we employ the metaphor we know, all the while realizing that while it captures some truth, it misses other truth. To be beloved is also to be pleasing, happy, satisfied, willing to accomplish a mission. This beloved status becomes more intense when one is chosen, selected, picked from others, preferred to the rest. Beloved status, in other words, is transformational; we change constantly in God's presence; we are in process of growth in the Spirit. Jesus became more spiritual. Those who encountered him entered more deeply into Spirit as they experienced him being changed throughout his mission. This impact affected them, and it affects us. Being a self-sacrificial beloved son or daughter plunges us into daily transformation.

Journal/Meditation: In what little ways does your beloved status transform you daily? In other words, how does your awareness of God's presence transform you into Spirit?

Prayer: Majestic Glory, you declared Jesus to be your Son, your Beloved, in whom you were well pleased on transfiguration's holy mountain. Grant that I may be transformed more into him by your Holy Spirit and accomplish the mission you have entrusted to me. Hear me through Jesus Christ my Lord. Amen.

Beloved Son: Vineyard Parable

Scripture: "[A vineyard owner] had still one other, a beloved son. Finally he sent him to [the tenants] saying, 'They will respect my son.'" (Mark 12:6)

Reflection: In Mark's Gospel, the vineyard parable (Mark 12:1–12) is, obviously, a retelling of the prophet Isaiah's song of the vineyard (Isa 5:1–7), and it serves as a summary or minia-ture presentation of Mark's Gospel. The author of Luke's Gospel rewrites the version of the analogy he found in Mark. While the author of Matthew's Gospel presents the analogy (Matt 21:33–46), he doesn't refer to the son as beloved. The son—Jesus—is beloved because God's voice declares him so at his baptism; because God's voice from the cloud declares him so at his transfiguration; and now because God's voice declares him so before his death. At the cross, the centurion will make this explicit. When the vineyard owner (God) refers to his Son (Jesus) as beloved, he is revealing the relationship that exists between them. It is the relationship that is more important than ownership of the vineyard, as manifested by the tenants, who are interested in the wealth the vineyard rep-resents. Matthew's Gospel's omission of the word *beloved* indicates that he understands the parable (analogy) from more of a business perspective.

Our relationships are, truly, our wealth. And we reveal those relationships in the way we describe them. While most of us do not use the word *beloved* often, we tell our beloveds that we love them. Those we identify as beloveds are, from our perspective, in-nocent, honorable, and spiritual. We love the beloveds not for who we are, but for who they are. Likewise, God doesn't love us for who we are, but for who he is! In the parable (analogy), the tenants kill the beloved son because they want to own the vineyard, and because they have no relationship with the vineyard owner other than being tenants. Among other messages, the vineyard parable illustrates the ugly example of how being a person full of divine love is not always easy. Certainly, the tenants didn't see the son as beloved; otherwise, they would not have killed him and thrown him out of the vineyard.

Journal/Meditation: Who is a beloved son or daughter to you? What affect has that relationship had on your love of him or her?

Prayer: Beloved Father, you sent your beloved Son into the vineyard of the world to collect responses to the grace you offer. After he was rejected and killed, you raised him from the dead so that I might come to a deeper understanding of your love. Fill me with the Spirit of love. Hear this prayer in the name of Jesus, your beloved Son, now and forever. Amen.

God's Beloved People 1

Scripture: ". . . [M]y beloved, be steadfast, immovable, always excelling in the work of the Lord, because you know that in the Lord your labor is not in vain." (1 Cor 15:58)

Reflection: In the CB (NT) the phrase "beloved [people]" is used multiple times. For example in his letter to the Romans, Paul refers to "all God's beloved in Rome, who are called to be saints" (Rom 1:7; 12:19). In addition to the above reference from Paul's First Letter to the Corinthians, he also addresses his readers as "my dear friends," that is, "my beloved" (1 Cor 10:14). The Corinthians are called "beloved" in Second Corinthians (7:1); in the same letter he tells his readers, "Everything we do, beloved, is for the sake of building you up" (2 Cor 12:19c). Repeatedly in his letter to the Philippians, he calls them beloved (Phil 1:12; 2:12; 3:13; 4:8). He even tells them that he loves and longs for them, who are his joy and crown, his beloved (Phil 4:1). Also repeatedly, in his First Letter to the Thessalonians, Paul refers to his readers as "beloved by God" (1 Thess 1:4), who "have become very dear" to him (1 Thess 2:8), urging them, the beloved (1 Thess 5:4, 14), to love one another more and more (1 Thess 4:9–10) and to pray for him (Paul) (1 Thess 5:25). Today, we would probably refer to all these folks as dear friends.

Paul writes to communities of believers, who, together, experience, explore, and grow in relationship with the Christ he preaches. He desires that his dear friends are united in their pursuit of their spiritual life in Christ. Furthermore, the apostle is calling his beloved to realize that they have been chosen by God and called to be saints. Thus, Gentiles, who receive Paul's letters, recognize that they are chosen, and they need to decide how they are going in live in response to their chosen status. By referencing his readers as God's beloved, Paul sets a standard of living for those

Gentiles chosen by God. Paul considers his readers to be his dear friends, those who are endeared to him because they are beloved of God. And Paul loves them dearly.

Journal/Meditation: Whom do you consider to be your beloved, your dear friends, people who are endeared to you? Make a list and pray for all those whose names you have written.

Prayer: Loving God, you call me to be one of your saints by living in your love. Keep me steadfast, immovable, and always excelling in your work. Grant that my labor may never be in vain, because it is guided by the Holy Spirit. In Jesus name I pray. Amen.

God's Beloved People 2

Scripture: ". . . [W]e must always give thanks to God for you, brothers and sisters, beloved by the Lord, because God chose you as the first fruits for salvation through sanctification by the Spirit and through belief in the truth." (2 Thess 2:13)

Reflection: In the CB (NT) we have genuine Pauline letters, those we know Paul wrote himself or those he dictated to a scribe or secretary. There are also letters that have Paul's name on them, but we know could not have been written by him because they can be dated after Paul's death in the mid-60s of the first century CE. These are referred to as second-generation Pauline letters; these are messages written by someone in Paul's name to answer questions and to deal with issues that had not yet arisen during Paul's lifetime. Among the second-generation Pauline letters are Second Thessalonians, First Timothy, and Second Timothy, to name a few. Since these letters were written in Paul's name, we find the same style and, often, the same vocabulary.

Thus, in the Second Letter to the Thessalonians, the author refers to the readers as "beloved by the Lord" and simply "beloved" (2 Thess 3:6; cf. 1 Tim 6:2). By the time these latter letters were written, the leaders of the next generation of believers had begun to establish guidelines for the chosen, "the first fruits for salvation through sanctification by the Spirit and through belief in the truth" (2 Thess 2:13). It is important to notice that God continues to choose people; in other words, the process continues. However, now God's chosen need to be sanctified, live by truth, confess faith, and stand against evil in order to be declared beloved of God. The free gift of God that Paul preached is already moving toward a reward earned through good behavior and right living. This development of the early church is not being critiqued; it is a natural development when Paul's expectation of Jesus' imminent return does not occur. We are no longer waiting for the Lord's return with imminent expectation; we are now in the long-range process of living our chosen status for a lifetime.

Journal/Meditation: What are your guidelines for living a Christian life?

Prayer: I give thanks to you, O God, because you chose me for salvation through sanctification by the Spirit and through belief in your truth. Grant me the grace to live into my status as one of your beloved children. I make this prayer in the name of Jesus, who is beloved by you now and forever. Amen.

God's Beloved People 3

Scripture: "Even though we speak in this way, beloved, we are confident of better things in your case, things that belong to salvation." (Heb 6:9)

Reflection: Besides Paul and second-generation Paul, there are numerous references in other letters in the CB (NT) to beloved. There is the reference in the Letter to the Hebrews above. The author of the Letter of James uses "my beloved" four times (Jas 1:16, 19; 2:5; 5:12) and "beloved" three times (Jas 5:7, 9, 10). The First Letter of Peter refers to the "beloved" two times (1 Pet 2:11; 4:12), and the Second Letter of Peter four times (2 Pet 3:1, 8, 14, 17). Even the one-chapter Letter of Jude uses the word three times (Jude 1:3, 17, 20). All these letter-writers attempt to convey fondness for the recipients of their letters, desiring that they be self-sacrificial—both senders and receivers.

These letters are less about a people chosen by God and more about a people who willingly live into God's love in the human

journey of highs and lows. The recipients of these letters are urged
to persevere through trials, to listen well, to pursue wisdom, to
practice patience, to be truthful, to abstain from sin, and to have
faith. The authors present a model for holiness and godly living.
In these letters, which represent an almost one-hundred-eighty-
degree turn from Paul, some believers may be falling away. The
writers exhort their readers to remain strong in the faith throughout their journey of life. When these authors address their readers
as beloved, they are employing a term of endearment, reminding
believers that they are affectionately loved. Hopefully, the readers,
the beloveds, will experience that love to be strong enough to keep
them strong in faith.

Journal/Meditation: Who have been the beloveds in your
life who have strengthened your faith? Make a list and identify
what each contributed to you.

Prayer: LORD God, through those who wrote to believers
in you and your Son, you convey your fondness for the recipients
of their letters. Help me in times of trial to be confident of better
things that come from salvation. Hear me through Jesus Christ,
who is Lord forever and ever. Amen.

God's Beloved People 4

Scripture: "Beloved, we are God's children now; what we will be
has not yet been revealed. What we do know is this: when he is
revealed, we will be like him, for we will see him as he is." (1 John
3:2)

Reflection: In addition to the use of beloved by Paul, second-
generation Paul, and other CB (NT) authors, there is the use by
the author of the First and Third Letter of John. In First John, the
author refers to his readers as beloved several times (1 John 2:7;
3:21; 4:1, 7, 11). Likewise, the author of the one-chapter Third
John calls his readers beloved (3 John 1:2, 5, 11). The key word
associated with Johannine writings is children, sometimes little
children (1 John 3:18). These authors consider their readers to be
dearest, precious, and cherished, just as any parent considers his

or her children treasured, prized, and highly regarded. The writers of these letters are functioning as parents caring for their children, who are immature in faith now, but will develop into disciples in the future. Like all children, who ultimately grow up, Johannine beloved children must choose to follow Jesus' path to God and imitate Jesus all along the way.

Also, in Johannine understanding, the beloved is a collective. In other words, the beloved are the members of the believing community. They form a group of precious believers, who are admired by the letter-writers and by other members in the community. The authors exhort community members, "God's children now" (1 John 3:2), to live in the light (1 John 2:7), to possess reassured hearts (1 John 3:19–22), not to believe every spirit, but to test them to be sure they are from God (1 John 4:1), to love one another (1 John 4:7, 11), to be in good health of body and soul (3 John 1:2), to continue to minister faithfully to friends in truth (3 John 1:3–5), and not to imitate what is evil, but to imitate what is good (3 John 1:11). All this advice is what parents give to their children in the community of the family.

Journal/Meditation: In what specific ways do you consider yourself a beloved child of God?

Prayer: Father, I am your child now, and what I will be you have not yet revealed. I trust that when it is revealed, I will be like you and see you as you are. As one of your beloved children, protect me and keep me safe as you did your only-begotten Son, Jesus Christ, who lives and reigns with you and the Holy Spirit, one God, forever and ever. Amen.

Beloved Children

Scripture: "I am not writing this to make you ashamed, but to admonish you as my beloved children." (1 Cor 4:14)

Reflection: In his First Letter to the Corinthians, Paul calls his readers beloved children; the person writing the Letter to the Ephesians in Paul's name tells his readers to "be imitators of God, as beloved children" (Eph 5:1). In both verses, the operative metaphor is the parent-child relationship. Children are imitators of their parents. While they may also look for guidance, wisdom, and correction, primarily they want to imitate their parents in relating, cooking, cleaning, and speaking, often sharing things in the presence of visitors that the parents prefer not be said in front of company! To be beloved children is to be dear to the apostle Paul, so dear that he practices tough love, admonishing his readers to better behavior, just like a parent disciplines his or her children. For Paul, starting a church is like having children; as the father of the family church in Corinth, Paul expects the members to imitate him, Christ, and God.

Being the parent of a church requires self-sacrificial love through letter-writing, mentorship, and admonishment along with offering guidance and wisdom. It is taking the phrase of the Lord's Prayer—"Your will be done, on earth as it is in heaven" (Matt 6:10b)—seriously. If we imitate God, we are in the process of overcoming worldly views, our egocentric thoughts, and our self-righteous agendas. God sees the whole world, knows all our thoughts, and knows that we are not capable of communication with him unless he wills it. In other words, while we are dear to God, we need to imitate the Holy One. And if we need help, we have plenty of assistants, like Paul, who remind us that we are beloved children, who need a little admonishment from time to time.

Journal/Meditation: What have you given up in order to imitate God? Explain.

Prayer: Father, through the apostle you direct me to imitate you. Grant me the wisdom of the Holy Spirit to know your will and to do it. Hear me in the name of Jesus, who lives and reigns with you now and forever. Amen.

Beloved Chosen Ones Called

Scripture: "As God's chosen ones, holy and beloved, clothe yourselves with compassion, kindness, humility, meekness, and patience" (Col 3:12)

Reflection: The author of the Letter to the Colossians is a second-generation Pauline writer who considers his readers called to relationship with God through Christ. The metaphor he employs is that of clothing. The unknown author wants his readers to dress themselves in the qualities of compassion, kindness, humility, meekness, and patience. In other words, those who are chosen and identified as holy and beloved are called to self-sacrifice in being set apart for Christ, willing to endure for his sake and the sake of the broader ministry, and committed to a Christ-like way of living.

Being called and chosen is a daunting task. We are clothed in a death wish. To be meek in a day and time when showing compassion can get you killed is, indeed, challenging. The Matthean Jesus begins his sermon on the mount with this beatitude: "Blessed are the meek, for they will inherit the earth" (Matt 5:5). This is not the small, quite, submissive person we usually associate with meekness. The Greek word for meek contains the connotation that one has a sword, knows how to use it, but keeps it in its scabbard. It is taming the monster of the self that desires to wield power. The meek yield such power because they are beloved, chosen; they have the power of God, but they do not exploit it. They use such power self-sacrificially for their good and the good of others. The meek wield the power of the sword while keeping it sheathed. In a similar vein, the author of the Letter of Jude addresses "those who are called, who are beloved in God the Father and kept safe for Jesus Christ" (Jude 1:1). Here, the author desires that his readers be protected from all harm. The task of Christianity is to be an adult while still being a beloved child; the challenge is to keep the two metaphors together.

Journal/Meditation: What do you need to do to tame your monster or to keep yourself in check to become even more a beloved chosen one kept safe and called to clothe yourself with meekness?

Prayer: Heavenly Father, your Son declared blessed those who are meek and announced that they would inherit the earth. As one of your beloved chosen ones, you have called me to adult love. Clothe me in the grace that strengthens me in your service through Jesus Christ my Lord. Amen.

Beloved Individuals

Scripture: "The brothers, both the apostles and the elders, to the believers of Gentile origin in Antioch and Syria and Cilicia, greetings.... [W]e have decided unanimously to choose representatives and send them to you, along with our beloved Barnabas and Paul, who have risked their lives for the sake of our Lord Jesus Christ." (Acts 15:23, 25–26)

Reflection: Not only are Barnabas and Paul referred to as beloved in the Acts of the Apostles passage above, but Paul is called "our beloved brother" by the author of the Second Letter of Peter (3:15). In his Letter to the Romans, Paul refers to the Jews as beloved (Rom 11:28); he also describes the following people as beloved: Epaenetus (Rom 16:5), Ampliatus (Rom 16:8), Stachys (Rom 16:9), Persis (Rom 16:12b), Timothy (1 Cor 4:17), and Philemon as "dear friend" (Phlm 1:1b). In second-generation Pauline correspondence, the author of the Letter to the Colossians, writing in the apostle's name, identifies as beloved Epaphras (Col 1:7), Tychicus (Col 4:7), Onesimus (Col 4:9), and Luke (Col 4:14). The Third Letter of John identifies Gaius as beloved (3 John 1:1), and the Book of Revelation refers to the "beloved city" (Rev 20:9). All of these are referred to as beloved because they sacrifice themselves for the sake of the Jesus movement. They share a kinship, a bond, a close connection in which sacrifice, even the cross, is necessary to develop and maintain relationships that have developed because of the ministry of Jesus.

All of these beloved have learned how to navigate life through the vast amounts of malevolence in the world, just like Jesus did. Paul went to prison. Timothy was jailed. Jews were persecuted. All of them remained strong through self-sacrificial love. That is what makes them beloved; they did not run away, protest, or feel sorry for themselves. The beloved voluntarily accepted the malevolence and transformed it into benevolence. To be a self-sacrificing beloved is voluntarily to accept the malevolence that will undoubtedly occur, pick up the cross, and transform it into benevolence. Thus CB (NT) authors love their co-ministers, who mirror God's love in Christ to the world. God's love is the way modeled by Jesus. Those who incarnate self-sacrificial love are, indeed, beloved. Each beloved individual represents the multiple shapes of divine love.

Journal/Meditation: As a beloved individual person, what malevolence have you transformed into benevolence?

Prayer: When I am confronted with all the evil in the world, LORD God, give me the wisdom to transform it into kindness and generosity that connects me to all your beloved children. Count me among those you name beloved through Jesus Christ, who is Lord forever and ever. Amen.

5

Love, God, Son, and Spirit

Faith Working Through Love

Scripture: ". . . [T]he only thing that counts is faith working through love." (Gal 5:6b)

Reflection: A relationship with God through Christ and energized by the Spirit is demonstrated by faith working through graced love. Justification is not attained through the works of the Law, according to Paul, but is offered as grace by God and demonstrated in loving acts by those who have accepted the Holy One's offer. Thus, love can only be known and expressed through faith that what God did in Jesus he will also do in us. God, the source of love, is known by faith, which works through love. In other words, faith is made effective through loving acts. Acts or works are not done to earn grace; they are done in order to demonstrate faith. The author of the Letter to the Ephesians refers to this as "love with faith" (Eph 6:23). The First Letter of Timothy refers to "the grace of our Lord [which] overflowed . . . with the faith and love that are in Christ Jesus" (1 Tim 1:14), as does the Second Letter of Timothy, which exhorts the reader to hold onto sound teaching "in the faith and love that are in Christ Jesus" (2 Tim 1:13). Self-sacrificial love manifested in acts demonstrates that a person has accepted God's offer of grace.

This idea can make a huge difference in the world today. Instead of creating ideological complexities that are divisive, like that found in the Letter to the Galatians where the community is divided over the issue of circumcision with those for it and those against it, Paul makes clear the only thing that matters is faith working through love. If we replace circumcision with immigration, abortion, or gun laws, we can see that the same dichotomy that was affecting the Galatians is still affecting us today. Faith working through love offers us freedom from divisiveness. Paul calls the Galatians to a faith that is greater than any ideology. Timothy holds faith from sound teaching that is all-encompassing, yet impenetrable by anything other than love. To have a faith that works through love not only displays the power and love of God through Christ to those around us, but it frees us from the yoke of division. Faith working through love transcends divisions, helps the individual to know his or her true self, and enriches the person with the love of God in Christ which transcends all divisions.

Journal/Meditation: How have you experienced faith working through self-sacrificial love in your life?

Prayer: God my Father, you bring peace to the world through love with faith in your Son, my Lord Jesus Christ. Increase your grace within me that my undying love for Christ may be manifested in self-sacrificial acts of love. I ask this through the same Jesus Christ now and forever. Amen.

Love: Miscellaneous

Scripture: "Grace, mercy, and peace will be with us from God the Father and from Jesus Christ, the Father's Son, in truth and love." (2 John 1:3)

Reflection: In the single chapter Second Letter of John, the author tells his readers that grace—God's undeserved gift of himself to people, mercy—receiving from God what they do not deserve or can earn, and peace—no longer being at war with God—will be with them from God the Father and from Jesus Christ in truth and love. Truth and love are key themes in Johannine literature. Truth describes the relationship of the Father and the Son, and love describes the relationship of believers to each other. The relationship that exists between the Father and the Son is one of unity. There is no untruth that exists in that relationship; it is one of pure, self-sacrificial love. The love that exists between believers should model that unity established in self-sacrificial love. Genuine love sparks truth that flows outward from the believer to the community of believers and connects them to the truthful love of Father and Son. In his First Letter to the Thessalonians, Paul puts it this way: "We always give thanks to God for all of you and mention you in our prayers, constantly remembering before our God and Father your work of faith and labor of love and steadfastness of hope in our Lord Jesus Christ" (1 Thess 1:2–3). At the end of his First Letter to the Corinthians he writes, "My love be with all of you in Christ Jesus" (1 Cor 16:24).

The work of self-sacrificial love in Christ Jesus is offering it to others. In so doing, a person demonstrates in truth his or her connection to the overflowing self-sacrificial love between God the Father and God the Son. He or she knows that any work of faith is a labor of love grounded in steadfastness of hope (Rom 5:1–5; 1 Cor 13:13; Gal 5:5–6; 1 Thess 5:8). However, through the labor of love, love grows; the more one shares it or gives it away, the more one grows deeper in knowledge and depth of insight to enhance spiritual discernment, especially in grace, mercy, and peace.

Journal/Meditation: In what specific ways have you grown in grace, mercy, and peace through self-sacrificial love?

Prayer: God my Father, I pray that my love may overflow more and more with knowledge and full insight to help me to determine what is best, so that in the day of Christ, your Son, I may be pure and blameless. Hear me through Jesus Christ in truth and love now and forever. Amen.

Love: Passing from Death to Life

Scripture: "We know that we have passed from death to life because we love one another. Whoever does not love abides in death." (1 John 3:14)

Reflection: Death and resurrection form what is arguably the oldest literary theme known to humankind. We see examples of this in Egyptian mythology, Mesopotamian mythology, biblical narratives, and modern movies. If we look at the stories of some of the most influential people of this century, many of them were in the constant process of death and rebirth. Some participated in this process through education, some through exercise, and some through rigorous conversation. These individuals were always pushing themselves to the point of uncomfortable being, and transforming this state into their new standard of being. They were dying and being reborn over and over again.

This idea also manifests itself in a CB (NT) analogy. The Johannine Jesus explains that a grain of wheat does not bear fruit unless it dies (John 12:24). Jesus lives this comparison through his birth, to his death, and to his resurrection. "Those who love their life lose it," he says, "and those who hate their life in this world will keep it for eternal life" (John 12:25). Passing from life to death to life is a scary process because we fear death. We experience dying at various stages of our lives, one being in the late teens or early twenties. It is often triggered by graduating from high school or college. We realize that we have to accept responsibility for ourselves, develop our individual selves, and care for others at the same time; many people become so afraid that they go into denial and never become self-individualized. However, if you are a person who has died willingly to youth, freedom, career, anything, then you know just how rewarding this process is. It develops your individual self. This is what Jesus meant by his teaching that love requires dying and that love brings about new life. It is through sacrificial love that we rise above death and truly live in incomprehensible divine love. This is the ultimate expression of love as exemplified by Jesus, who lived, died, and entered into new life. If we continue this process of life, death, and life throughout our lives, we bear much fruit for eternal life.

Journal/Meditation: How has your capacity to love been transformed by your experiences of love, death, and new life?

Prayer: Father, Jesus, your Son, has taught me that unless a grain of wheat falls into the earth and dies, it remains just a single grain; but if it dies, it bears much fruit. Grant that I may be like the wheat grain, dying and rising to new life in your presence in union with Jesus Christ now and forever. Amen.

Spirit of Love

Scripture: "I appeal to you, brothers and sisters, by our Lord Jesus Christ and by the love of the Spirit, to join me in earnest prayer to God on my behalf." (Rom 15:30)

Reflection: There is Spirit (as in Holy Spirit) and there is spirit (as in an individual's spirit, the spirit of celebration, or the spirit of giving). When Paul appeals to the Romans by the love of the Spirit, he is referring to the divine dynamic force that flows from the Father and the Son, namely, the Spirit, who is self-sacrificial love poured into human hearts and resulting in the spiritual fruits of love, joy, peace, patience, kindness, generosity, faithfulness, gentleness, and self-control (Gal 5:22–23). In the words of the Second Letter to Timothy, the gift of the Holy Spirit results in a spirit of power and of love and of self-discipline in the individual (2 Tim 1:7). A person who has received the love of the Spirit is able to love in the Spirit (Col 1:8) and recognizes spiritual love manifested in his or her words and acts of love and, simultaneously, recognizes that fornication, impurity, licentiousness, idolatry, sorcery, enmities, strife, jealousy, anger, quarrels, dissensions, factions, envy, drunkenness, carousing, and other such things are not acts of love but of evil (Gal 5:19–21). The love of the Spirit spills over into our individual spirits and is manifested in self-sacrificial love.

There is, then, a circle of self-sacrificial love: Father, Son, and believers in the Spirit. They constitute a fellowship. In other words, love is a form of existence; the individual spirit reveals the Holy

Spirit, who is the love between the Father and the Son. Love of all types manifests the Spirit loving you, you loving the Spirit, and you living in a spirit of love through the Spirit of love. This melding together of Spirit and spirit into an enriching—yet paradoxical—existence is where we find the Spirit of love and the spirit of love.

Journal/Meditation: In what specific way have you experienced the union of your spirit and the Holy Spirit? What were the results?

Prayer: Father of our Lord Jesus Christ, through the Holy Spirit, you have given me a spirit of power and love and self-discipline. Draw me ever deeper into prayer that my spirit may remain united to your Spirit through your Son, Jesus Christ, who lives in love with you and the Holy Spirit, one God, forever and ever. Amen.

6

Growing in Love

Love What Cannot be Seen

Scripture: "Although you have not seen [Jesus Christ], you love him; and even though you do not see him now, you believe in him and rejoice with an indescribable and glorious joy . . . ." (1 Pet 1:8)

Reflection: The verse above from the First Letter of Peter raises this question: How do we love what we cannot see? Because we are human, we experience self-sacrificial love in what we do see, hear, taste, touch, and feel with another person. And yet the author of First Peter calls us fleshy humans to a higher level. We might call this a philosophical- or academic-like quality to agape love; it is a love without seeing. Maybe the closest we can get to understanding what First Peter is all about is to reflect upon a mature relationship that we have or have had. That developed relationship made us aware not only of the love of the other person, but it made us aware of divine love all around. In other words, we are able to abstract from the specific experience at least an idea of what unseen, self-sacrificial love for Jesus may be like. Using a Pauline image, by loving the other members of the body of Christ, we are loving Jesus, and by loving Jesus, we are loving the members of the body; they are one and the same.

Another way to attempt to grasp the meaning of loving one we have never seen is to look at conscious love. Conscious love, that is, a love anchored in awareness, is an exercise of the will. Self-sacrificial conscious love is a decision. Self-sacrificial conscious love is a deliberate choice. Out of the love of the One we have never seen, we become aware of our need to do the loving thing, just like we sacrifice ourselves for the one we love and can see. Just to ask the question—What is the loving thing to do?—indicates aware-ness of our belief that another loves us. Self-sacrificial love has the power to transform us, to change us, and to deepen our faith in the One we love unseen. Thus, even though we have never seen Jesus, we love him, and, like any other deep, self-sacrificial love relation-ship we have, we rejoice with indescribable and glorious joy!

Journal/Meditation: How has the love of a person—living or dead—that you no longer see continue to transform you? What comparisons exist between the love of that unseen person and the love you have for the unseen Jesus?

Prayer: Heavenly Father, even though I cannot see you, I love you. Likewise, I have not seen your Son, Jesus Christ, but I love him, and I believe in him. Hear my rejoicing with indescribable and glorious joy as praise of you, Father, Son, and Holy Spirit, now and forever. Amen.

Showing Great Love

Scripture: Jesus said to Simon the Pharisee: ". . . I tell you, her sins, which are many, have been forgiven; hence she has shown great love. But the one to whom little is forgiven, loves little." (Luke 7:47)

Reflection: The author of Luke's Gospel presents two Jew-ish outcasts who show great, self-sacrificial love. One of them is the prostitute, who brings an alabaster jar of ointment and anoints Jesus' feet with it. After Jesus' host, Simon the Pharisee, criticizes her activity, the Lukan Jesus declares that her many sins have been forgiven; her response is a demonstration of great, self-sacrificial love, displaying the honor and respect toward Jesus that his host did not present. This woman was not invited and was certainly out of place at this dinner. According to Simon, her presence and actions are seen as inappropriate and unacceptable, but that didn't stop her from expressing her great love. The other Jewish outcast is not even a Jew; he is a Roman centurion, whom the Jewish elders in Capernaum declare worthy of having Jesus heal his slave because the centurion loves the Jewish people and built their synagogue (Luke 7:4–5). Because Jesus finds faith—that he cannot find in Israel!—in the centurion, Jesus heals his slave. The centurion displays respect, caring, and love for people, no matter what their belief may be. Not only does he seek healing for his servant from a Jewish Jesus, but he, uncharacteristically, built a synagogue for the Jews in Capernaum. Thus, he shows great, self-sacrificial love.

Both the prostitute and the centurion are presented as models for Luke's Gentile audience. The woman shows humility by washing Jesus' feet and using her hair to dry his feet. She unselfishly uses her own fragrant oil to anoint Jesus' feet. We are challenged to love in a similar manner—without limits, without fear, and without concern for what others think. The centurion models those who refuse to judge those who are different; he treats all—slave and Jew—equally. He chooses to love self-sacrificially even though this could lead easily to judgment by his superiors. We are challenged by these two great lovers to love in the same way, regardless of gender, race, ethnicity, religion, social class, sexual orientation, economic class, or any other. This type of self-sacrificial love is dangerous, risky, and, yet, it is the most inclusive, fulfilling, and powerful way to be transformed.

Journal/Meditation: In what specific ways have you shown great love? To whom did you show it?

Prayer: Almighty God, I express my great love for you this day because you have cancelled the great debt of my sin through the death and resurrection of Jesus, your Son. Fill me with your Spirit of love that I may forgive others as you have forgiven me through the same Christ my Lord. Amen.

Love to be Noticed

Scripture: Jesus said, ". . . [W]henever you pray, do not be like the hypocrites; for they love to stand and pray in the synagogues and at the street corner, so that they may be seen by others. Truly I tell you, they have received their reward." (Matt 6:5)

Reflection: A hypocrite is a person who gives a false appearance of having admirable principles, beliefs, or feelings. Both the Matthean and Lukan Jesus are merciless toward such a person. In his Sermon on the Mount in Matthew's Gospel, Jesus tells his listeners not to imitate hypocrites, who pray so that others may see them praying, because they are not really praying; they merely look like they are praying. Later, the Matthean Jesus identifies the scribes and Pharisees as hypocrites who "love to have the place of honor at banquets and the best seats in the synagogues" (Matt 23:6). Luke records Jesus damning the Pharisees who "love to have the seat of honor in the synagogues and to be greeted with respect in the marketplaces" (Luke 11:43), and telling his followers to "[b]eware of the scribes, who like to walk around in long robes, and love to be greeted with respect in the marketplaces, and to have the best seats in the synagogues and places of honor at banquets" (Luke 20:46). In John's Gospel, the narrator states that the Pharisees "loved human glory more than the glory that comes from God" (John 12:43).

Self-sacrificial love has to be authentic; it cannot be only an appearance. Hypocrites appear as if they are praying out of self-sacrificial love, but the only reward they get is the attention they receive. Their actions are selfish rather than altruistic, full of emptiness rather than rich in love, and meaningless in the eyes of God. Likewise, scribes and Pharisees appear to be authentic, but they seek only their own honor, respect, and power. They fail to understand the self-sacrificing love to which God calls them. When we pray, our prayer should be a self-sacrificial action that furthers the development of our relationship with God. When we are in a position of leadership, power, fame, or wealth, our self-sacrificial love motivates us to care for others, not worrying about where we sit, what we wear, or where we shop. Being aware of the hypocrite trap helps us to pursue a sincere and authentic relationship with God that overflows in self-sacrificial love toward others.

Journal/Meditation: Who are you when no one is looking? How is your self-sacrificial love authentically demonstrated in prayer and daily life?

Prayer: Father, grant me a self-sacrificial love that comes from your glory rather than human glory. Keep me from all hypocrisy that my principles, beliefs, and feelings will be true and aligned with the teaching of your Son, Jesus Christ, who is Lord forever and ever. Amen.

The World's Love

Scripture: Jesus said to his disciples, "If you belonged to the world, the world would love you as its own. Because you do not belong to the world, but I have chosen you out of the world—therefore the world hates you." (John 15:19)

Reflection: Friendship love with the world is not possible for a follower of Jesus according to John's Gospel. In Johannine literature the world, from which people need to be rescued, is contrasted with heaven, the goal of those who follow Jesus. Disciples do not belong to the world; they belong to heaven. If they did belong to the world, it would not hate them; it would relate to them in a brotherly or sisterly manner. However, Jesus has chosen them out of the world, that place which "loves and practices falsehood," according to the Book of Revelation (22:15). The First Letter of John is even more emphatic in its statement about the world. Using agape, the author writes: "Do not love the world or the things in the world. The love of the Father is not in those who love the world" (1 John 2:15). In other words, self-sacrificing love is not compatible with the world; furthermore, the Father's love cannot be in those who love the world because such love is not compatible with him.

There can be no doubt that the world is full of pleasures, temptations, and instant gratification that create a false reality in which there is no human growth toward maturity. In other words, the world lulls us into complacency. The world's love is false; it is concerned only about the present moment. Agape love is focused on the future; it draws us forward to even greater love. Followers of Jesus have been chosen out of the world, even though they still have to live in it. We are to love God more than the world; our love is not to be divided. Counter-cultural living and self-sacrificing suggests we are doing well when culture dislikes us, and we should be concerned when culture accepts us. If the counter-cultural example of Christ is to be our model, then, as we follow him, we will appropriately butt heads with the present day culture just as he did.

Journal/Meditation: Do you love the world? Do you live a counter-cultural life? Why? Why not?

Prayer: Father, your Son, Jesus, has revealed that your love is not in those who love the world. Because he has chosen me out of the world, fill me with your grace of perseverance to live a counter-cultural life until I reach heaven, where you live and reign as one God—Father, Son, and Holy Spirit—forever and ever. Amen.

Walk According to Love

Scripture: "If your brother or sister is being injured by what you eat, you are no longer walking in love." (Rom 14:15)

Reflection: Every day most people get from one place to another by walking, the basic form of human transportation. According to Paul in his Letter to the Romans, walking in love is a way of life that puts others first; the self is sacrificed for the good of others. In Paul's letter, the matter of unclean or clean food reminds us to be considerate of our brothers and sisters and be mindful not to let the freedom in our belief, perspective, or thought cause them to struggle in their faith. In other words, walking in self-sacrificial love is so integrated into our being that it automatically builds up those who pursue it (1 Cor 14:1; 1 Tim 6:11; 2 Tim 2:22) and possess it (1 Cor 8:1) so that they do everything in love (1 Cor 16:14). It flows out of us, and it is integral as breathing. According to the Second Letter of John, ". . . [T]his is love, that we walk according to [Jesus'] commandments; this is the commandment just as you have heard it from the beginning—you must walk in it" (1 John 1:6).

While we challenge our brothers and sisters on the same journey of faith that we are on, we do so appropriately and only out of love. While pursuing and living love reveal our relationship with God, it also presents our true identity in Christ. This spurs us to reject greed, controversies, and quarrels because they do not build up others. Walking in love means knowing God, the source of love, and traveling with him, while meeting the needs of our brothers and sisters along the way. Christians should strive for agreement in the essentials of faith and grace. The most essential thing to agree upon is the foundation of agape love for everyone. Out of this walk, we see that we can have differences of belief and at the same time remain free in Christ to walk in love while focused on the good of others.

Journal/Meditation: In the past month, how have you walked in love? Make a list of your specific experiences of sacrificing yourself for the good of others.

Prayer: Father, you have revealed the edifying power of self-sacrificial love in the life, death, and resurrection of your Son. Guide my steps in pursuit of such love that I may walk in it all the days of life. I ask this in the name of Jesus Christ, who is Lord forever and ever. Amen.

Love in Truth

Scripture: ". . . [S]peaking the truth in love, we must grow up in every way into him who is the head, into Christ." (Eph 4:15)

Reflection: According to the Second Letter to the Thessalonians, there are people "who are perishing, because they refused to love the truth and so be saved" (2 Thess 2:10). The second-generation Pauline Letter to the Ephesians urges us to speak the truth in love, while the author of the Second Letter of John identifies himself as an elder who loves in truth the elect lady (2 John 1:1), and the author of Third Letter of John identifies himself as an elder who loves in truth Gaius (3 John 1:1). What these texts suggest is that we speak the truth about what we believe out of self-sacrificial love. Our truth—about the Father, the Son, and the Holy Spirit—is subjective, and we present it to others out of love for their consideration. However, there is another level of truth that is generally fluid and much larger. This level of truth would include such things as the earth being part of a solar system, which is itself a part of a universe of which there are billions. People are connected in the broader level of truth, while those who share Christianity, Judaism, or Islam are connected in a narrower level of truth. From the perspective of the Christian Scriptures, all Christians are connected through their knowledge of Jesus Christ, their belief in him as savior, their relationship with him and the Father, and their obedience to his commands.

Thus, Christians grow in truth and speak the truth more as they abide in Christ. The challenge presented in the present is living the narrower level of truth without being judgmental, narrow minded, or condemning others. The task is to remain faithful to our definition of truth in the midst of relativity. The task is to stand for truth spoken in love, when truths appear to be contradictory or in opposition to each other. It is very shallow to love only those who agree with us and to reject those who disagree. Instead of fearing what lies beyond well-defined Christian truth, in love we come to see that we exist within the broader level. Our discomfort with not having God and our lives in a neat, well-defined box or dogma cannot in love stop us from discovering the truth of others; otherwise we become a living contradiction producing rejection and hatred of those who believe differently. When the understanding of truth becomes static and limiting, the experience of speaking truth in love is non-existent.

Journal/Meditation: In what recent experience have you spoken truth in love? Did you recognize the limitation of your truth? Explain.

Prayer: Father, I desire to speak the truth about your Son in love so that with other believers I will grow up in every way into him who is the head: Christ Jesus. Give me a great respect for all truth, and grant that one day I may know eternal truth in your kingdom forever and ever. Amen.

Genuine Love

Scripture: "I [, Paul,] do not say this as a command, but I am testing the genuineness of your love against the earnestness of others." (2 Cor 8:8)

Reflection: Several times in his Second Letter to the Corinthians Paul expresses his desire that love be genuine. He tells his readers to reaffirm their love for someone who has caused them pain (2 Cor 2:8). It is with genuine love that the apostle commends himself to the Corinthians (2 Cor 6:6), and he asks them to receive those who are sent to them "openly before the churches," and "show them the proof of [their] love" (2 Cor 8:24). Indeed, the aim of all instruction is love that comes from a pure heart (1 Tim 1:5). Thus, "Christ may dwell in [their] hearts through faith, as [they] are being rooted and grounded in love" (Eph 3:17). In other words, love is to be sincere, genuine, real, and authentic. We are called to love others with genuine love in order for our love to be perceived as certain, unconditional, self-sacrificial, and freely given. Such love is displayed when there is no self-gain, manipulation, or limiting link to behavior.

Genuine love emanates from the core of one's being, which is God. Therefore, real love is God making himself known through our sincere expression of love, thus communicating the character and identity of God, who is love. Genuine love triumphs conditionality because it is selfless, self-sacrificial, and other-worldly. We can exist in a state of genuine love that originates from divine presence when we are in communion with the divine. When we become so aware of love that it becomes a part of the fiber of our being, then we enter the realm of genuine love: we become rich by becoming poor; it does not matter how much we have, but how much we give; and we need only to speak the truth in love without judgment or condemnation. Once our entire being has

LOVE ADDICT

been changed, then we can grasp what genuine love really is: God's power, faith, and joy alive and at work within us.

Journal/Meditation: If genuine love is a process, does it ever end? Is there a stage of fully matured love? If there is, what is it? If there is not, why continue to grow in love?

Prayer: Genuinely loving God, your Son, Jesus Christ, dwells in my heart through faith, as I am rooted and grounded in love. With the guidance of the Holy Spirit, keep my love sincere, genuine, and authentic now and forever. Amen.

In Love

Scripture: "Blessed be the God and Father of our Lord Jesus Christ, who has blessed us in Christ with every spiritual blessing in the heavenly places, just as he chose us in Christ before the foundation of the world to be holy and blameless before him in love." (Eph 1:3–4)

Reflection: To be "in love" is an idea often skewed by our culture's romanticized presentation of love. We often think of love as a burning romance between people who face many perils, but always stick together. While this portrayal may occur in the world, being in love is often far from that perfect. If we never get past the Hollywood meaning of love, then we can never understand how to be "in love"—how to set an example in love (1 Tim 4:12), how to proclaim Christ out of love (Phil 1:16), and how to be united in love (Col 2:2).

Self-sacrificial love brings people together; it has the power to unify and to empower a new generation as a result of the latest generation living in love. Everything is brought together, held together, and made complete in God's love manifested in Christ and his love. We are to live this love selflessly and generously. It is one thing to know of someone, and it is another to know someone. The former is a limited understanding; the latter is an experience of being in relationship with someone. The experience of being in love, living in a love relationship, is far richer and more meaningful. It is only through agape love that we are able to experience the

74

fullness of love. In Christ we are in love, connected to everything and everyone. To be in love is to be aware of love surrounding us, the same love we disperse into the world. To be in love is to live in the divine power that breathed life into all.

Journal/Meditation: In what specific ways do you live in love?

Prayer: Heavenly Father, you desire that our hearts be encouraged and united in love so that we may have all the riches of assured understanding and all the knowledge of your mystery. Send the Holy Spirit to draw my spirit deeper into your love that I may be united with you, Father, Jesus Christ, and Holy Spirit, forever and ever. Amen.

Increase in Love

Scripture: ". . . [M]ay the Lord make you increase and abound in love for one another and for all, just as we abound in love for you." (1 Thess 3:12)

Reflection: The wish expressed by Paul in his First Letter to the Thessalonians that they increase and abound in love is echoed later in the same letter when the apostle appeals to his readers to esteem very highly in love those who labor among them (1 Thess 5:13). Such agape love is so important that the author of the Book of Revelation criticizes the Ephesians because they "have abandoned the love [they] had at first" (Rev 2:4). Likewise, he tells the Laodiceans that he reproves and disciplines those he loves (Rev 3:19), although the word used here is philia, friendship, brotherly, or sisterly love. While the examples from the Book of Revelation may appear dark when contrasted with those from the First Letter to the Thessalonians, they present a great insight as to how we can increase in love, as well as how God's hand is at work in that process. Once we become aware that we live in love, we are forced to decide to continue to grow in love or to turn a blind eye to the divine reality that has been made clear to us. The consequence of willful blindness is ultimate dissolution into chaos. God disciplines those he loves, not out of spite, but out of love. God wants nothing more for us than to know love in its purest form, even if it can only be experienced in glimpses.

We are challenged to increase and abound in love toward one another and all people as God does for us. This love demonstrates appreciation, patience, attention to individual needs, and looking for the best in each other as we strive to increase in love. To increase in love is not only to be aware of love, but to be aware of the discipline present in it. In order to increase our being in love, God may motivate us through the allowance of hardship or prune us to direct new growth. He may tell us to die and then raise us. As a result, our very being will increase in love until it reaches ultimate maturity. Thus, while philia love is hopeful, encouraging, supportive, and filled with understanding, it is also accountable.

Journal/Meditation: Over the past few years how have you increased and abounded in love? Give specific examples.

Prayer: Lord God, keep me accountable to my life in your Son, Jesus Christ, by making me increase and abound in love for you and for all. I ask this in the name of my Lord Jesus Christ now and forever. Amen.

Continue in Love

Scripture: ". . . [Women] will be saved through childbearing, provided they continue in faith and love and holiness . . . ." (1 Tim 2:15)

Reflection: While we may not agree with the context—such as childbearing saves women—we must agree that continuing in self-sacrificial love is a theme presented in the CB (NT). In his First Letter to the Corinthians, Paul asks his readers, "What would you prefer? Am I to come to you with a stick, or with love in the spirit of gentleness?" (1 Cor 4:21) Second generation Paul, as seen above in the First Letter to Timothy, and as found in the Letter to Titus continue this theme. Titus is exhorted, "Tell the older men to be temperate, serious, prudent, and sound in faith, in love, and in endurance" (Titus 2:2). Even in old age we are to continue in self-sacrificial love. Thus, love is to be enduring in every stage of life and in all aspects of life. Love, or loving, is a process that will never be complete as long as we are living on the earth.

Our mission is to imitate Christ and set a godly example for others through a life lived in self-sacrificial love. Mature love, the ultimate form of love, is a never-ending process of growth and development. Because it is always in process, it cannot be described adequately. In other words, at the end of the day we have only a vague idea of what this form of love looks like. The only thing we can do is strive towards this conceptualized idea through the process of continuing in self-sacrificial love. Some people may become stagnant in love, oblivious to the power that love carries through its continuance in people in the world. Without acting, without continuing, in self-sacrificial love we do not experience the power that manifests itself when we continue in love. As we grow in love, our awareness continually grows as well; we become aware of the self-sacrificial love that surrounds us. To continue in love means to become gentle, yet strong. It means to know that you have a sword—a stick for Paul—but to keep it sheathed—a spirit of gentleness for Paul. When we continue in love, we live in that in-between state of knowing love yet continuing in it, being gentle yet being strong.

Journal/Meditation: How are you continuing in self-sacrificial love? Give specific examples.

Prayer: God of love, the self-sacrificial love of your Son, Jesus Christ, serves as an enduring example for all people. With the guidance of the Holy Spirit make me sound in love yet ever-growing in love with you now and forever. Amen.

Love Life

Scripture: ". . . [Our comrades] have conquered [the accuser] by the blood of the Lamb and by the word of their testimony, for they did not cling to life even in the face of death." (Rev 12:11)

Reflection: Loving life is not the same as clinging to it. John of Patmos declares that those who love life do not cling to it even in the face of death. They love life enough to let it go. When we love life, people notice. This noticeable, ripple effect is what allows one life-loving individual to have an impact on others. As we live out of love, we pursue peace in our actions and words, leaving behind kindness instead of giving into evil. Loving life well means we are willing to die for someone or a cause greater than ourselves. Sacrificial love demonstrates that love transcends this life. To suffer, struggle, or be persecuted for Christ-like sacrificial love means one has chosen relationship with Christ over one's own life. One has chosen self-sacrificial love whatever the cost and is not willing to compromise to hold on to one's own life.

The author of the First Letter of Peter offers some advice on loving life. He states, "Those who desire life and desire to see good days, let them keep their tongues from evil and their lips from speaking deceit" (1 Pet 3:10). Basically, desiring life is loving life, and the key to loving life is developing the individual so that he or she avoids evil. When each person connects to the divine, grows by calling others to grow, accepts responsibility for himself or herself, develops ways to articulate thoughts, and controls emotions, then the person's reality is transformed and he or she begins to love life. Once you truly love life, then you can fully cooperate with the divine presence that guides you constantly. Basking in that presence is where we can find the life-giving force of love, begin to love life, and experience good days. Risk is embraced in agape love, acceptance is attained, and we do whatever it takes to maintain integrity, character, and belief in spite of threat to personal safety, persecution, or condemnation from others.

Journal/Meditation: To whom does your love of life flow? How has sacrificial love changed you and the person to whom it flows?

Prayer: LORD God, keep my tongue from evil and my lips from speaking deceit. Grant my desire for a loving life with good days, but do not let me cling to life, even in the face of death, in imitation of your Son, Jesus Christ, who lives and reigns with you and the Holy Spirit, one God, forever and ever. Amen.

Love of Money

Scripture: ". . . [T]he love of money is a root of all kinds of evil, and in their eagerness to be rich some have wandered away from the faith and pierced themselves with many pains." (1 Tim 6:10)

Reflection: It is very common for people to say incorrectly that money is the root of all evil. However, the author of the First Letter to Timothy states clearly that it is the love of money—not money itself—that is the root of all kinds of evil. Money is simply a medium of exchange necessary to make purchases and sales of the things necessary for living in this life. We have to have money to survive; it gets us food, shelter, vehicles, public transportation, and runs charities. The love of money speaks about the motives of one's heart. Desiring money above the love for God, self, and others leads one away from that which truly matters. The verse from First Timothy is no different than other texts concerning any other idol. Our ultimate concern is our god, and the biblical authors know that. Because money can be a driving force, an ultimate concern, the love of money can lead people away from putting God first in their lives.

The author of the Letter to the Hebrews exhorts his readers to keep their lives "free from the love of money" and to be content with what they have (Heb 13:5a). In contentment, we know and trust that God is always with us and will never forsake us. We do not look to money to satisfy us or be our source of contentment; we find contentment in a relationship with the divine. The love of the divine will not fail, and a heart that is fixed on the divine—instead of distracted by money—will experience a deepening relationship with the God who is always with us. This God wants nothing more than to love and be loved by us. A healthy, friendly love of money may result in a successful life on earth, but money cannot buy our entrance into eternal love with God.

Journal/Meditation: What is your perspective on money and its use?

Prayer: O God, you have given me money to facilitate my life on earth. With the Holy Spirit direct my heart that money not become the object of my love and that you remain always the One I love above all things. Grant me contentment now and eternal life in the kingdom where you are one God—Father, Son, and Holy Spirit—living in love now and forever. Amen.

Love's Kiss

Scripture: ". . . [T]he betrayer [, Judas,] had given [the crowd] a sign, saying, 'The one I will kiss is the man; arrest him and lead him away under guard.' So when he came, he went up to [Jesus] at once and said, 'Rabbi!' and kissed him." (Mark 14:44–45)

Reflection: The author of Matthew's Gospel relies upon his Markan source to narrate Judas's betrayal of Jesus with a kiss (Matt 26:48–49), usually given to each cheek. A kiss is a greeting, a good-bye, an acknowledgment of friendship, and a sign of affection or love. The author of Luke's Gospel alters his Markan source to imply that Judas does not kiss Jesus (Luke 22:47–48); nevertheless, Judas betrays Jesus. The Greek word translated kiss is *philia* or friendship love. Judas betrays his friendship with Jesus with the very sign that represents it! Judas is loved by Jesus, but that love is not reciprocated. If Jesus is the ultimate sign of divine love manifested on earth, then Judas's kiss becomes a sign of his false self. Friendship love is not always reciprocated, and sometimes it may cause suffering to the one offering it. Jesus loved Judas, but Judas did not love Jesus.

Luke's Gospel presents another type of kiss. An unnamed woman, identified as a prostitute (sinner) (Luke 7:37), enters an all-male dinner party to find Jesus. "She stood behind him at his feet, weeping, and began to bathe his feet with her tears and to dry them with her hair. Then she continued kissing his feet and anointing them with [an alabaster jar of] ointment" (Luke 7:38). Jesus tells his host, Simon the Pharisee, that he gave Jesus no kiss, but the woman has not stopped kissing his feet (Luke 7:45); she shows great sisterly love to Jesus (Luke 7:47). She does not hold back in expressing her love, but gives honor and respect to Jesus through her actions. She stands as a contrast to Judas, who was not changed by Jesus' love. The unnamed, anointing woman was changed. Jesus loved both of them, but only one returned his love. Like Jesus, love's kiss may not always be exchanged, but we can always give others the kiss of love.

Journal/Meditation: What does a kiss mean to you? When has love's kiss not been reciprocated in your life, and how did this impact you?

Prayer: Father of Jesus, the woman who anointed and kissed the feet of your Son showed great love unlike Judas, who betrayed him with a kiss. With the Spirit of love fill me with genuine friendship love for others that it may flow outward into the world. Grant this through Jesus Christ my Lord. Amen.

Cold Love

Scripture: Jesus said, ". . . [B]ecause of the increase of lawlessness, the love of many will grow cold." (Matt 24:12)

Reflection: In Matthew's Gospel, Jesus speaks about one's love for God growing cold over time due to the increase in wickedness. The author of the Second Letter to Timothy identifies a certain Demas, who is "in love with this present world" and has deserted Paul (2 Tim 4:10). John's Gospel records Jesus telling the Jews, ". . . I know that you do not have the love of God in you" (John 5:42). Self-sacrificial love is difficult and challenging to keep in the midst of many different earthly circumstances. However, we are only as strong as our love. One's ministry is only as strong as one's love. A relationship is only as strong as one's love. Divine cooperation is only as strong as one's love. If self-sacrificial love grows cold, we can find ourselves in a stronghold from which it is nearly impossible to escape.

Cold love is loveless. Cold love is an abandonment of awareness of the divine presence. Thus, there are two distinct aspects to cold love; one of them is losing one's ability to love self-sacrificially at all. We know that love is growing cold when our ability to love deeply decreases. The other aspect of cold love is a shift away from living in awareness of the divine presence. When we stray from God, we can find ourselves being loveless. True self-sacrificial love becomes cold love very rapidly. All that we are left with is chaos and bitterness towards the world. This state of being is dangerous, as it leads to hatred and, ultimately, evil behavior. It may be easier for love to grow cold when people begin to believe that they have earned love or deserve it, becoming blind to their unrighteousness and need for a relationship with God and others. However, it is more difficult for love to grow cold when we realize how much we have been forgiven (Luke 7:42).

Journal/Meditation: Has your self-sacrificial love ever grown cold? If not, why not? If so, how did you restore it?

Prayer: All-loving God, you demonstrate the power of self-sacrificial love in the incarnation of your Son, Jesus Christ. Direct my heart to the divine, warm love he revealed, and keep me steadfast in it now and forever. Amen.

Without Love

Scripture: "You must understand this, that in the last days distressing times will come. For people will be lovers of themselves, lovers of money, . . . inhuman." (2 Tim 3:1–3)

Reflection: The Greek word *storge* is translated into English as *inhuman* in the above passage from the Second Letter to Timothy. This is one of only three occurrences of the word in the CB (NT). In Romans 1:31, the same word is translated as *heartless*. Instead of agape or philia, storge is used to describe natural, family love, the special affection between parents and children and husbands and wives. In Second Timothy and Romans, the word attempts to name those without love, those who are unloving. The third use of storge is also found in Paul's Letter to the Romans, but in a positive sense. Paul exhorts the Romans: "Let love be genuine; love one another with mutual affection" (Rom 12:9a, 10a). Here, Paul applies the natural, family love to God's family, the community of believers.

There can be little doubt that we live in a heartless and inhuman world. It is easy to walk by the homeless on our city streets and feel no pity or kindness because, actually, we fail to see them or we see them and don't have time for them. Likewise, it is easy to show great cruelty to the creatures who share the earth with us by poaching, killing only for the sport, or slaughtering for various body parts, such as horns, because they sell for lots of money. Yes, everywhere we look we see behavior that is not becoming of human beings. However, we can see the love that manifests itself as mutual affection. There are those who serve the homeless in shelters, soup kitchens, and clothing stores. There are those who take ecological stewardship seriously, trying to protect natural resources and the animals who share those with us. They bring endangered species to reserves to save their lives. The love that is usually shared among family members seeps out into the world and can restore heart and humanity to those on the edge of God's family.

Journal/Meditation: Have you ever found yourself inhuman or heartless? Explain. How did you regain mutual affection?

Prayer: Father, when the last days of distressing times come and inhuman and heartless people seem to dominate the earth, strengthen my mutual affection for all the people and creatures and earth you have created. Keep me faithful through Jesus Christ my Lord. Amen.

Perfect Love

Scripture: "Love has been perfected among us in this: that we may have boldness on the day of judgment, because as [God] is, so are we in this world. There is no fear in love, but perfect love casts out fear; for fear has to do with punishment, and whoever fears has not reached perfection in love." (1 John 4:17–18)

Reflection: According to the author of the First Letter of John, God is perfect, self-sacrificial love, and as we live in him, we experience this perfect self-sacrificial love that he has to offer. Through a life lived in love, we have intimacy and relationship with God as he lives in us and we live in him. Perfect, self-sacrificial love is the ultimate, greatest, divine, all-encompassing, or fully-mature love. Perfect love creates communion, fellowship, or oneness and a peace that drives out anxiety and fear. This is the kind of love that we strive to reach, but can never fully grasp.

From an attachment perspective, there is healthy bonding in this self-sacrificial love, and it creates safety, security, and comfort. A healthy attachment is created between a parent and a child. As a child experiences love from a parent, the whole being of that child is impacted and transformed by this love. This gives the child the secure foundation that is necessary to reciprocate love to another, to be vulnerable, to trust, and to explore the world and relationships securely and with curiosity. As adults, we continue to get glimpses into perfect, divine love through our Spirit-filled experiences during private prayer or corporate worship, which result in a communion between God and us. We may experience perfect love in art, music, nature, or friends. Greater awareness on our part makes it easier to glimpse perfect love. Thus, perfect love is sharing the gift of self with another or others and receiving the gift of another, a process that is grounded in God.

Journal/Meditation: What relationship do you have that gives you a glimpse of perfect love?

Prayer: All-loving God, those who abide in love abide in you, and you abide in them. Fill me with your perfect love and remove whatever fear remains in me. Hear me in the name of the Son whom you loved through death to new life. Amen.

Bibliography

Lee, Matthew T., Margaret M. Poloma, and Stephen G. Post. *The Heart of Religion: Spiritual Empowerment, Benevolence, and the Experience of God's Love.* New York: Oxford University Press, 2013.

Myers, Jacob D. *Making Love with Scripture.* Minneapolis: Fortress, 2015.

Polan, Gregory. "Final Address to the Congress of Abbots." *AIM USA* 26:2 (2017) 3.

Rohr, Richard. "Breach-Menders." Center for Action and Contemplation. December 24, 2017. http://cac.org.

——. "Irreplaceable 'Thisness.'" Center for Action and Contemplation. March 18, 2018. http://cac.org.

Roman Missal, The: Study Edition. Collegeville, MN: Liturgical, 2012.

Shea, John. *To Dare the Our Father: A Transformative Spiritual Practice.* Collegeville, MN: Liturgical, 2018.